SPORT ROYAL *AND OTHER STORIES*

BY

ANTHONY HOPE

CHAPTER I.
The Sequel to the Ball.

HEIDELBERG seems rather a tourist-ridden, hackneyed sort of place to be the mother of adventures. Nevertheless, it is there that my story begins. I had been traveling on the Continent, and came to Heidelberg to pay my duty to the castle, and recruit in quiet after a spell of rather laborious idleness at Homburg and Baden. At first sight I made up my mind that the place would bore me, and I came down to dinner at the hotel, looking forward only to a bad dinner and an early bed. The room was so full that I could not get a table to myself, and, seeing one occupied only by a couple of gentlemanly looking men, I made for it, and took the third seat, facing one of the strangers, a short, fair young man, with a little flaxen mustache and a soldierlike air, and having the other, who was older, dark, and clean-shaved, on my left. The fourth seat was empty.

The two gentlemen returned my bow with well-bred negligence, and I started on my soup. As I finished it, I looked up and saw my companions interchanging glances. Catching my eye, they both looked away in an absent fashion, each the while taking out of his pocket a red silk handkerchief and laying it on the table by him. I turned away for a moment, then suddenly looked again and found their eyes on me, and I fancied that the next moment the eyes wandered from me to the handkerchiefs. I happened to be carrying a red handkerchief myself, and, thinking either that something was in the wind or perhaps that my friends were having a joke at my expense (though, as I said, they looked well-bred men), I took it out of my pocket and, laying it on the table, gazed calmly in front of me, my eyes naturally falling on the fair young man.

He nodded significantly to the older man, and held out his hand to me. I shook hands with him, and went through the same ceremony with the other.

"Ah!" said the young man, speaking in French, "you got her letter?"

I nodded.

"And you are willing?"

The first maxim for a would-be adventurer is always to say "yes" to questions. A "no," is fatal to further progress.

"Yes," I answered.

"It will be made worth your while, of course," he went on.

I thought I ought to resent this suggestion.

"Sir," I said, "you cannot possibly mean to suggest——"

The young man laughed pleasantly.

"My dear fellow," he said, "ladies have their own ways of paying debts. If you don't like it——" and he shrugged his shoulders.

"Oh," said I, smiling, "I misunderstood you."

"It is, of course," said the older man, speaking for the first time, and in a loud whisper, "of vital importance that His Royal Highness' name should not appear."

This really began to be mysterious and interesting. I nodded.

"That goes without saying," said the young man. "And you'll be ready?"

"Ready!" I said. "But when?"

"Didn't I tell you? Oh, six o'clock to-morrow morning."

"That's early hours."

"Well, you must, you know," he answered.

"And," added the older man, "the countess hopes you'll come to breakfast afterward at ten."

"I'll be there, never fear," said I, "and it's very kind."

"Bravo!" said the young man, clapping me on the shoulder (for we had risen from table). "You take it the right way."

As may be supposed, I was rather puzzled by this time, and decidedly vexed to find I should have to be up so early. Still, the mention of His Royal Highness and the countess decided me to go on for the present; probably the real man—for, unless it were all a mad joke, there must be a real man—would appear in the course of the evening. I only hoped my new friends would, in their turn, take it in the right way when that happened.

"Have you a servant with you?" asked the young man, as we said good-night.

"No," said I; "I am quite alone."

"You are a paragon of prudence," he answered, smiling. "Well, I'll call you, and we'll slip out quietly."

Just as I was getting into bed, the waiter knocked at my door and gave me a note. It bore no address.

"Is it for me?" I asked.

"Yes, sir," he answered. "You are the gentleman who dined with Herr Vooght and M. Dumergue?"

I supposed I was, and opened the note.

"You are generous and forgiving, indeed," it said (and said it in English). "What reward will you claim? But do be careful. He is dangerous.—M."

"The devil!" I exclaimed.

The next morning I was aroused at five o'clock by my two friends.

"Good-morning, Herr Vooght," said I, looking just between them.

"Good-morning," answered the older man.

"Now, my dear fellow, come along. There's a cup of coffee downstairs," said the other, whom I took to be Dumergue.

After coffee, we got into a close carriage with a pair of horses, and drove two or three miles into the country; my companions said little. Dumergue twice asked in a joking way how I felt, and Vooght puzzled me very much by remarking:

"They are bringing all the necessaries; but I don't know what they will choose."

When this was said, Dumergue was humming a tune. He went on for five minutes, and then said, with a touch of scorn:

"My good Vooght, they know our friend's reputation. They will choose pistols."

I could not repress a start. No doubt it was stupid of me not to have caught the meaning of this early expedition before, but it really never struck me that our business might be a duel. However, so it seemed, and apparently I was one of the principals. Dumergue noticed my little start.

"What's the matter?" he asked.

"Do they know my name?" said I.

"My dear friend, could you expect the baron to fight with an unknown man? The challenge had to be in your name."

I had clearly been the challenger. I was consumed with curiosity to know what the grievance was, and how the countess was concerned in the matter.

"The countess assured us," said Vooght, "that she had your authority."

"As fully as if I had been there," I answered, and Dumergue resumed his tune.

I was sincerely glad that the name of my original had been given, for his reputation for swordsmanship had evidently saved me from a hole in my skin. I was a fair hand with a pistol; but, like most of my countrymen, a mere bungler with the rapier. It was very annoying, though, that my friends' exaggerated prudence prevented them mentioning my name: it would have been more convenient to know who I was.

I had not long for reflection, for we soon drew up by a roadside inn, and, getting out of the carriage, walked through the house, where we were apparently expected, into a field behind. There were three men walking up and down, and two of them at once advanced to meet Vooght and Dumergue. I remained where I was, merely raising my hat, and the third man—a big, burly fellow, with a heavy black mustache—followed my example.

This one, no doubt, was the baron. To be frank, he looked a brute, and I had very little hesitation in assuming that the merits of the quarrel must be on my side. I was comforted by this conclusion, as I had no desire to shoot an unoffending person. Preliminaries were soon concluded. I overheard one of the baron's representatives mention the word apology, and add that they would meet us halfway, but Dumergue shook his head decisively. This defiant attitude became Dumergue very well; but I, for my part, should have been open to reason.

The baron and I were placed opposite one another at twelve paces. There were to be two shots—unless, of course, one of us were disabled at the first fire; after that, the seconds were to consider whether the matter need go further.

The word was just about to be given, when to my surprise the baron cried:

"Stop!"

Everyone looked at him in astonishment.

"Before we fire," he went on, "I wish to ask this gentleman one question. No —I will not be stopped!"

His seconds, who had advanced, fell back before his resolute gesture, and he continued, addressing me:

"Sir, will you do me the honor to answer one question? Are you the person who accompanied——"

Vooght struck in quickly:

"No names, please!"

The baron bowed, and began again.

"On your honor, sir, are you the gentleman who accompanied the lady in question to the masked ball on the night in question?"

These gentlemen were all diplomatic. I thought I would be diplomatic too.

"Surely this is grossly irregular?" I said, appealing to my supporters.

"I ask for an answer," said the baron.

"It's nothing but a new insult," said I.

"I have my reasons, and those gentlemen know them."

This was intolerable.

"You mean to fight, or you don't, M. le Baron," said I. "Which is it?"

He shrugged his shoulders.

"Your master is well served," he said with a sneer.

His seconds looked bewildered: Vooght bit his nails, and Dumergue swore furiously, and, coming near me, whispered in my ear:

"Shoot straight! Stop his cursed mouth for him!"

I had not the least intention of killing the baron, if I could avoid it without being killed myself; but I thought a slight lesson would improve his manners, and, when the word came, I fired with a careful aim. He evidently meant mischief, for I heard his ball whiz past my ear; I missed him clean, being much out of practice, and, I dare say, rather nervous. I pulled myself together for the second shot, for I saw that my opponent was not to be trifled with, and I should not have been the least surprised to find myself in paradise the next moment. On the word I fired; the baron fell back with a cry, and simultaneously I felt a tingle in my left hand, and the unmistakable warm ooze of blood. The witnesses ran to my opponent, and raised his head. Dumergue turned round to me:

"Are you hurt?"

"A scratch," I answered, for I found the ball had run up my arm, merely grazing me in its passage.

A hurried consultation followed; then Vooght and Dumergue raised their hats and joined me.

"We had best be off," said Vooght.

"Is he dead?" I asked.

"No," said Dumergue, with a little disappointment, I thought. "He'll get over it; but he's safe for a week or two. Not a bad shot, colonel!"

So I was a colonel!

"Now," said Vooght, "we'll drive back, and send you to the countess."

I had made up my mind to get away from the place as soon as I could, but my curiosity to see the *causa belli* was too strong, and I said I should be delighted to keep my engagement.

Dumergue smiled significantly, and Vooght hurried us into the carriage. We drove back to the town, and then two or three miles into the country again, till we came to a pretty villa, embowered in trees, and standing some two hundred yards back from the road. There was no drive up to the house, a turf walk forming the passage from the highway. Vooght motioned me to get down.

"Don't you accompany me?" I asked.

Dumergue smiled again.

"Oh, no!" he said. "Come for us at the hotel, and we'll all be off by the two o'clock train."

"Unless you are detained," added Vooght.

"I shouldn't be detained, if I were you," said Dumergue dryly. "Who knows? The baron may die!"

I was quite determined not to be detained, and said so. I was also quite determined not to keep the rendezvous at the hotel, but to slip away quietly by myself. The colonel might arrive at any moment.

I watched my friends drive off, and then walked briskly up to the house. A man in livery met me before I had time to ring.

"Are you the gentleman?" he asked.

I nodded.

"Will you be so kind, sir, as to walk straight in? That door, sir. The countess expects you."

I had my doubts about that, but I walked in, shutting the door swiftly behind me, lest the servant should hear anything. I thought an explosion not improbable.

The room was dim, close curtains shutting out the growing strength of the sunshine. The air was thick with the scent of flowers that overpowered without quite smothering the appetizing smell rising from a table profusely spread for breakfast. I had entered softly, and had time to take note of the surroundings before I became aware of a tall, slight figure in white, first moving impetuously toward me, then stopping abruptly in surprise. Presumably, this was the countess. Charming as she was, with her open blue eyes, fluffy golden hair, and fresh tints, I wondered from what noble house she sprang. However, the fountains of honor are many, and their streams meander sometimes through very winding channels.

The countess stood and looked at me. I bowed and smiled.

"You are naturally surprised," I said, in my smoothest tone.

"I was expecting—another gentleman."

"Yes, I know. I come in his place."

"In his place?" she repeated, in incredulous tones.

"Yes; in the colonel's place."

"Hush!" she exclaimed. "We needn't mention names."

It suited me perfectly not to mention names.

"I beg pardon," I murmured.

"But how is it possible?" she asked. "Do you know what he was to come for?"

"Oh, yes!"

"And he hasn't come?"

"No."

She frowned.

"Wouldn't he come?"

"He couldn't. So I came."

"But how did you know anything about it? Did he tell you about the pr—about the affair?"

"No. I only heard——"

"From him?"

"Yes—that you wanted a champion."

"Oh, that's absurd! Why, you never heard of me!"

"Ah, indeed I have!"

"And—did you recognize me under my new name?"

"Your——"

"My—my title. You know."

"The—he told me that. Must I confess? I jumped at the chance of serving you."

"You had never seen me!"

"Perhaps I had seen your photograph."

She smiled at this, but still looked perturbed.

"Pray don't be distressed," said I. "I am very discreet."

"Oh, I hope so! The prince she spoke in a whispe was so urgent about discretion. You haven't seen him?"

"The prince? No."

"And—when is it to be?"

"I don't quite understand." This was my first truthful remark.

"Why, the duel!"

"Oh, it's all over!"

"Over!"

"Yes—two hours ago."

"And the baron? No, forgive me. You! Are you hurt?"

"Not a bit. He's hurt."

"Is he dead?" she asked breathlessly.

"I am sorry, countess. Not quite. Was that necessary?"

"Oh, no! Though he deserved it. He insulted me shamefully."

"Then he did deserve it."

She went off at a tangent.

"What became of my letter?"

"They gave it to me. You only said for the gentleman who dined with your friends."

"Then you read it?" she asked, blushing.

"Yes. How I wish I were the rightful owner of it!"

"Why didn't he come?" she asked again.

"He's going to write and explain."

"And you really came because——"

"May I tell you already? Or have you guessed already?"

She blushed again.

"I don't see what else the prince could do, you know," she said. "He ought, of course, never to have gone to the ball at all."

"Perhaps not," I answered; "but I suppose he was tempted."

"Do you think very badly of me?"

"I should think you perfection if——"

"Well?"

"You would give me some breakfast."

"Oh, what a shame! You're starving! And after all you have done! Come, I'll wait on you."

My meal was very pleasant. The lady was charming; she satisfied every feeling I had, except curiosity. She was clearly English; equally clearly she was involved with some great people on the Continent. I gathered that the baron had insulted her, when she was with the prince, and the latter could not, whether for state or domestic reasons, espouse the quarrel. So far I got, but no farther.

"What a debt I owe you!" she said, as she led the way after breakfast to the top of a little tower. An awning was spread overhead, and armchairs on the floor. A cool breeze blew, and stirred her hair.

"I am more than paid!"

"Fancy, if you had been hurt!"

"Better I than the colonel!" I suggested.

She darted a smile at me.

"Oh, well," she said, "you came, and he didn't. I like you best."

It was all very charming, but time was flying, and I began to plan a graceful exit.

"You make it hard to go," I said.

"Yes, I suppose we must go as soon as possible. Herr Vooght said at two o'clock."

I was startled. Delightful as she was, I hardly reckoned on her being one of the party.

"The prince will be so pleased to see you," she went on.

"Will he?"

"Why, you will have my recommendation!"

"I'm sure it must be all-powerful!"

"But we have two hours before we need start. You must want to rest."

"What a charming tower this is!"

"Yes; such a view. Look, we can see for miles. Only I hate that stretch of dusty road."

I looked carelessly toward the road along which we had come.

"Look what a dust!" she said. "It's a carriage! Oh, they'll upset!"

I jumped up. About half a mile off, I saw a carriage and pair driven furiously toward the villa. My heart beat.

"Who can it be?" she said.

"Don't be frightened," said I. "Possibly the authorities have found out about the duel."

"Oh!"

"Let me go and see."

"Take care!"

"And in case I have to slip away——"

"I shall go alone. You will join us?"

"Yes. But now, in case——"

"Well?"

"As a reward, may I kiss your hand?"

She gave it me.

"I am glad you came," she said. "Stay, perhaps it's only our friends coming for us."

"I'll go and see."

I was reluctant to cut short our good-by,—for I feared it must be final,—but no time was to be lost. With another kiss—and upon my honor, I can't swear whether it was her hand or her cheek this time—I rushed downstairs, seized my hat and cane, and dived into the shrubberies that bordered on the turf walk. Quickly I made my way to within twenty yards of the road, and stopped, motionless and completely hidden by the trees. At that moment the carriage, with its smoking horses, drew up at the gate.

Dumergue got out; Vooght came next; then a tall, powerful man, of military bearing. No doubt this was the colonel. They seemed in a hurry; motioning the driver to wait, they walked or almost ran past me up the path. The moment they were by me and round a little curve, I hastened to the gate, and burst upon the driver.

"A hundred marks to the station!"

"But, sir, I am engaged."

"Damn you! Two hundred!" I cried.

"Get in," said he, like a sensible man, bundling back the nose-bags he was just putting on his horses. I leaped in, he jumped on the box, and off we flew quicker even than they had come. As we went, I glanced up at the tower. They were there! I saw Vooght and Dumergue lean over for a moment, and then turn as if to come down. The tall stranger stood opposite the lady, and seemed to be talking to her.

"Faster!" I cried, and faster and faster we went, till we reached the station. Flinging the driver his money, I took a ticket for the first train, and got in, hot and breathless. As we steamed out of the town, I saw, from my carriage-window, a neat barouche with a woman and three men in it, driving quickly along the road, which ran by the railway. It was my party! Youth is vain, and beauty is powerful. I bared my head, leaned out of the window, and kissed my hand to the countess. We were not more than thirty yards apart, and, to my joy, I saw her return my salutation, with a toss of her head and a defiant glance at her companions. The colonel sat glum and still; Vooght was biting his nails harder than ever; Dumergue shook his fist at me, but, I thought, more in jest than in anger. I kissed my hand again as the train and the carriage whisked by one another, and I was borne on my way out of their reach.

CHAPTER II.
At the Hôtel Magnifique.

TO a reflective mind nothing is more curious than the way one thing leads to another. A little experience of this tendency soon cured me of refusing to go anywhere I was asked, merely because the prospects of amusement were not very obvious. I always went—taking credit of course for much amiability—and I often received my reward in an unexpected development of something new or an interesting revival of a former episode. It happened, a few months after my adventure at Heidelberg, that my brother's wife, Jane Jason, asked me, as a favor to herself, to take a stall at the theater where a certain actress was, after a long and successful career in the provinces, introducing herself to a London audience. Jane is possessed by the idea that she has a keen nose for dramatic talent, and she assured me that her *protégée* was a wonder. I dare say the woman had some talent, but she was an ugly, gaunt creature of forty, and did not shine in Juliet. At the end of the second act I was bored to death, and was pondering whether I knew enough of the play to slip out without Jane being likely to discover my desertion by cross-examination, when my eye happened to fall on the stage-box in the first tier. In the center seat sat a fair, rather stout man, with the very weariestexpression that I ever saw on human face. He was such an unsurpassed impersonation of boredom that I could not help staring at him; I could do so without rudeness, as his eyes were fixed on the chandelier in the roof of the house. I looked my fill, and was about to turn away, and go out for a cigarette, when somebody spoke to me in a low voice, the tones of which seemed familiar.

"Ah, impostor, here you are!"

It was Dumergue, smiling quietly at me. I greeted him with surprise and pleasure.

"How is the baron?" I asked.

"He cheated the—grave," answered Dumergue.

"And the countess?"

"Hush! I have a message for you."

"From her?" I inquired, not, I fear, without eagerness.

"No," he replied, "from the prince. He desires that you should be presented to him."

"Who is he?"

"I forgot. Prince Ferdinand of Glottenberg."

"Indeed! He's in London, then?"

"Yes, in that box," and he pointed to the bored man, and added:

"Come along; he hates being kept waiting."

"He looks as if he hated most things," I remarked.

"Well, most things are detestable," said Dumergue, leading the way.

The prince rose and greeted me with fatigued graciousness.

"I am very much indebted to you, Mr. Jason," he said, "for——"

I began to stammer an apology for my intrusion into his affairs.

"For," he resumed, without noticing what I said, "a moment's bewilderment. I quite enjoyed it."

I bowed, and he continued.

"The only things I cling to in life, Mr. Jason, are a quiet time at home and my income. You have been very discreet. If you hadn't, I might have lost those two things. I am very much obliged. Will you give me the pleasure of your company at supper? Dumergue, the princess will be delighted to see Mr. Jason?"

"Yes, sir, Her Royal Highness will be delighted," answered Dumergue.

"Where was the princess going?" asked the prince.

"To a meeting of the Women's International Society for the Promotion of Morality, at the Mansion House, sir."

"*Mon Dieu!*" said the prince.

"His Majesty is much interested in the society, sir."

"I am sure my brother would be. Come along, Mr. Jason."

The prince and princess were staying at the Hôtel Magnifique in Northumberland Avenue. We drove thither, and were told that the princess had returned. Upon further inquiry, made by Dumergue, it appeared that it would be agreeable to her to sup with the prince and to receive Mr. Jason. So we went into the dining room and found her seated by the fire. After greeting me, she said to the prince:

"I have just written a long account of our meeting to the king. He will be so interested."

She was a small woman, with a gentle manner and a low, sweet voice. She looked like an amiable and intelligent girl of eighteen, and had a pretty, timid air, which made me wish to assure her of my respectful protection.

"My brother," said the prince, "is a man of catholic tastes."

"It is necessary in a king, sir," suggested Dumergue.

The prince did not answer him, but offered his arm to his wife, to escort her to the table. She motioned me to sit on her right hand, and began to prattle gently to me about the court of Glottenberg. The prince put in a word here and there, and Dumergue laughed appreciatively whenever the princess' descriptions were neat and appropriate—at least, so I interpreted his delicate flattery.

I enjoyed myself very much. The princess was evidently, to judge from her conversation, a little Puritan, and I always love a pretty Puritan. That rogue Dumergue agreed with all her views, and the prince allowed his silence to pass for assent.

"We do try at court," she ended by saying, "to set an example to society; and, as the king is unmarried, of course I have to do a great deal."

At this moment, a servant entered, bearing a card on a salver. He approached the princess.

"A gentleman desires the honor of an audience with Her Royal Highness," he announced.

"At this time of night!" exclaimed the princess.

"He says his business will not bear delay, and prays for a interview."

"All business will bear delay," said the prince, "and generally be the better for it. Who is he?"

"The Baron de Barbot."

"Oh, I must see him," cried the princess. "Why, he is a dear friend of ours."

I had detected a rapid glance pass between Dumergue and the prince. The latter then answered:

"Yes, we must see Barbot. If you will go to the drawing room, I'll take your message myself."

"That is kind of you," said the princess, retiring.

"Give me the card," said the prince, "and ask the baron to be kind enough to wait a few minutes."

The servant went out, and the prince turned to me.

"Why didn't you kill him, Mr. Jason?" he asked.

"Is it——" I began.

"Yes, it's your baron," said Dumergue.

"It's really a little awkward," said the prince, as though gently remonstrating with fate. "We had arranged it all so pleasantly."

"It would upset the princess," said Dumergue.

"What upsets the princess upsets me," said the prince. "I am a devoted husband, Mr. Jason."

"If there is anything I can do, sir," said I, "rely on me."

"You overwhelm me," said the prince. "Is there anything, Dumergue?"

"Why, yes, sir. Mr. Jason was at the ball. Why should he have fought, if he wasn't?"

"You are right, Dumergue. Mr. Jason, you were at the ball."

"But, sir, I—I don't know anything about the ball."

"It was just like other balls—other masked balls," said Dumergue.

"Perhaps a little more so," added the prince, lighting a cigarette.

"There was a scandal at the last one," Dumergue continued, "and the king strictly forbade anyone connected with the court to go, under pain of his severe displeasure. There had been a rumor that a royal prince was at the one before, and consequently——"

"That royal prince was specially commanded not to go to this one," said the prince.

"It was bad enough," resumed Dumergue, "that it should be discovered that the princess' favorite lady-in-waiting, the Countess von Hohstein——"

"Who bore such a high character," interjected the prince.

"Did go, and, moreover, went under the escort of an unknown gentleman—a gentleman whose name she refused to give."

"Was that discovered?" said I.

"It was. This baron detected her, and, with a view, as we have reason to believe, to compelling her companion to declare himself, publicly insulted her."

"Whereupon," said the prince, "you very properly knocked him down, Mr. Jason."

"I beg your pardon, sir?"

"The princess," continued Dumergue, "was terribly agitated and annoyed at the scandal and the duel which followed. And of course the countess left the court, and returned to England."

"To England?"

"Yes; she was a Miss Mason. The king ennobled her at the princess' request."

I smiled and said:

"And now there is a question about who her escort was?"

"There is," said Dumergue. "It is believed that the baron entertains an extraordinary idea that the gentleman in question was no other than——"

"Myself," said the prince, throwing away his cigarette.

I remembered the baron's strange questions before the duel.

"Dispose of me as you please, sir," said I.

"Then you were at the ball, and knocked the baron down!" exclaimed Dumergue.

"A thousand thanks," said the prince.

"But what are we to do with him now, sir?" asked Dumergue. "The princess will be expecting him."

"I will go and tell the princess of Mr. Jason's confession. You go with Mr. Jason, and tell the baron that the princess cannot receive him. I want him to see Mr. Jason."

"But, sir," said I, "I didn't fight under my own name."

The prince was already gone, and Dumergue was halfway down the stairs. I followed the latter.

We found the baron in the smoking room, taking a cup of coffee. A couple of men sat talking on a settee near him; otherwise the room was empty.

Dumergue went up to the baron, I following a step or two behind him. The baron rose and bowed coldly.

"I am charged," said Dumergue, "to express His Royal Highness' regrets that Her Royal Highness cannot have the pleasure of receiving you. She has retired to her apartments."

"The servant told me she was at supper."

"He was misinformed."

"I'm not to be put off like that. I'll have a refusal from the princess herself."

"I will inform His Royal Highness."

The baron was about to answer, when he caught sight of me.

"Ah, there's the jackal!" he said, with a sneer.

I stepped forward.

"Do you refer to me?" I asked.

"Unless I am wrong in recognizing my former antagonist, Colonel Despard."

This was just what I had anticipated. Dumergue did not seem surprised either.

"Of course it is Colonel Despard," he said. "You would not be likely to forget him, baron."

We had been speaking in a low tone, but at Dumergue's sneer, the baron lost his temper. Raising his voice, he said, almost in a shout:

"Then I tell Colonel Despard that he is a mean hound."

If I assumed the colonel's name, I felt I must at least defend it from imputations. I began:

"Once before, baron, I chastised——"

I was interrupted. One of the men on the settee interposed, rising as he spoke.

"I beg pardon, gentlemen, but is it Colonel Despard of the Hussars to whom you refer?"

"Yes," said the baron.

"Then that gentleman is not Colonel Despard," announced our new friend. "I am Colonel Despard's brother-in-law."

For a moment I was at a loss; things were falling out so very unfortunately. Dumergue turned on the stranger fiercely:

"Pray, sir, was your interposition solicited?"

"Certainly not. But if this gentleman says he is Colonel Despard, I take leave to contradict him."

"I should advise you to do nothing of the sort," said I. "M. Dumergue knows me very well."

"This person," said the baron, "passed himself off as Colonel Despard, and, by that pretext, obtained from me the honor of a duel with me. It appears that he is a mere impostor."

The other man on the settee called out cheerfully, "Bob, send for the police!"

Dumergue looked rather sheepish; his invention failed him.

"Do either or both of these gentlemen," said I, indicating the baron and the colonel's brother-in-law, "call me an impostor?"

"I do," said the baron, with a sneering laugh.

"I am compelled to assert it," said the other, with a bow.

I had edged near the little table, on which the baron's coffee had been served. I now took up the coffee-pot and milk-jug. The coffee I threw in the baron's face, and the milk in that of his ally. Both men sprang forward with an oath. At the same moment, the electric light went out, and I was violently pulled back toward the door, and someone whispered, "Vanish as quick as you can. Go home—go anywhere."

"All right, sir," said I, for I recognized the prince's voice. "But what are they doing?"

"Never mind; be off." And the prince handed me a hat.

I walked quickly to the door, and hailed a hansom. As I drove off, I saw the prince skip upstairs, and a *posse* of waiters rush toward the smoking room. I went home to bed.

The next morning, as I was breakfasting, my man told me two gentlemen were below, and wished to see me. I told him to show them up, and the prince and Dumergue came in, the former wrapped up in a fur coat, with a collar that hid most of his face.

"The prince would like some brandy in a little soda water," said Dumergue.

I administered the cordial. The prince drank it, and then turned to me.

"Did you get home all right?" he asked.

"Perfectly, sir."

"After you took leave of us, we had an explanation. Mr. Wetherington—it was Mr. Wetherington at whom you threw the milk—was very reasonable. I explained the whole matter, and he said he was sure his brother-in-law would pardon the liberty."

"I'm afraid I took rather a liberty with him."

"Oh," said Dumergue, "we made him believe the milk was meant for the baron, as well as the coffee. I said we took it *au lait* at Glottenberg."

"It's lucky I thought of turning out the light," said the prince. "I was looking on, and it seemed about time."

"What did the hotel people say, sir?"

"They are going to sue the electric company," said the prince, with a slight smile. "It seems there is a penalty if the light doesn't work properly."

"And the baron, sir?"

"We kicked the baron out as a blackmailer," said Dumergue. "He is going to bring an action."

"I return to Glottenberg to-day," concluded the prince; "accompanied by the princess and M. Dumergue."

I thought this course very prudent, and said so. "But," I added, "I shall be called as a witness."

"No; Colonel Despard will."

"Well, then——"

"He will establish an *alibi. Voilà tout!*"

"I am glad it all ends so happily, sir."

"Well, there is one matter," said the prince. "I had to tell the princess of your indiscretion in taking Mme. Vooght——"

"Who, sir?"

"Mr. Jason," put in Dumergue, "has not heard that the countess and Vooght are married."

"Yes," said the prince, "they are married, and will settle in America. Vooght is a loss; but we can't have everything in this world."

"I hope Herr Vooght will be happy," said I.

"I should think it very unlikely," said the prince. "But, to return. The princess is very angry with you. She insists——"

"That I should never be presented to her again?"

"On the contrary; that you should come and apologize in person. Only on condition of bringing you again could I make my peace for bringing you once."

I was very much surprised, but of course I said I was at the princess' commands.

"You don't mind meeting us in Paris? We stay there a few days," said Dumergue.

"You see," added the prince, "Dumergue says there are things called writs, and——"

"I will be in Paris to-morrow, sir."

"I shall be there to-day," said the prince, rising.

CHAPTER III.
The Mission of the Ruby

I COULD not imagine why the princess desired to see me. It would have been much more natural to punish the impertinence of which I had no doubt been guilty—I mean, of which it was agreed on all hands that I had been guilty—by merely declining to receive me or see me again. Even the desire for a written apology would have been treating me as of too much account. But she wanted to see me. What I had heard of the princess' character utterly forbade any idea which ought not to have been, but would have been, pleasant to entertain. No; she clearly wanted me, but what for I could not imagine.

When I went to claim my audience, the prince was not visible, nor Dumergue either, and I was at once received by the princess alone. She was looking smaller, and more simple and helpless than ever. I also thought her looking prettier, and I enjoyed immensely the pious, severe, forgiving little rebuke which she administered to me. I humbly craved pardon, and had no difficulty in obtaining it. Indeed, she became very gracious.

"You must come to Glottenberg," she said, "in a few months' time."

"To obey Your Royal Highness' commands will be a delightful duty," said I, bowing.

She rose and stood by the fire, "toying" (as the novelists say) with her fan.

"You seem to be an obliging man, Mr. Jason," she said. "You were ready to oblige Mme. Vooght."

I made a gesture of half-serious protest.

"I wonder," she continued, "if you would do me a little service."

"I shall be most honored if I may hope to be able to," said I. What did she want?

She blushed slightly, and, with a nervous laugh, said:

"It's only a short story. When I was a young girl, I was foolish enough, Mr. Jason, to fall in love, or at least to think I did. There was a young English *attaché*—I know I can rely on your perfect discretion—at my father's court, and he—he forgot the difference between us. He was a man of rank, though. Well, I was foolish enough to accept from him a very valuable ring—a fine ruby—quite a family heirloom. Of course, I never wore it, but I took it. And when I married, I——"

She paused.

"Your Royal Highness had no opportunity of returning it?"

"Exactly. He had left the court. I didn't know where he was, and—and the post was not quite trustworthy."

"I understand perfectly."

"I saw in the papers the other day that he was married. Of course I can't keep it. His wife ought to have it—and I dare not—I would prefer not to—send it."

"I see. You would wish me——"

"To be my messenger. Will you?"

Of course I assented. She went into an adjoining room, and returned with a little morocco case. Opening it, she showed me a magnificent ruby, set in an old gold ring of great beauty.

"Will you give it him?" she said.

"Your Royal Highness has not told me his name?"

"Lord Daynesborough. You will be able to find him?"

"Oh, yes!"

"And you will—you will be careful, Mr. Jason?"

"He shall have it safely in three days. Any message with it, madame?"

"No. Yes—just my best wishes for his happiness."

I bowed and prepared to withdraw.

"And you must come and tell me——"

"I will come and make my report."

"I do not know how to thank you."

I kissed her hand and bowed myself out, mightily amused, and, maybe, rather touched at the revelation of this youthful romance. Somehow such things are always touching, stupid as they are for the most part. It pleased me to find that the little princess was flesh and blood.

She followed me to the door, and whispered, as I opened it:

"I have not troubled the prince with the matter."

"Wives are so considerate," thought I, as I went downstairs.

On arriving in England, I made inquiries about Lord Daynesborough. I found that it was seven years since he had abruptly thrown up his post of *attaché*, without cause assigned. After this event, he lived in retirement for some time, and then returned into society. Three months ago he had married Miss Dorothy Codrington, a noted beauty, with whom he appeared much in love, and had just returned from his wedding tour and settled down for the season at his house in Curzon Street. Hearing all this, I thought the little princess might have let well alone, and kept her ring; but her conduct was no business of mine, and I set about fulfilling my commission. I needed no one to tell me that Lady Daynesborough had better, as the princess would have phrased it, not be troubled with the matter.

I had no difficulty in meeting the young lord. In spite of the times we live in, a Jason is still a welcome guest in most houses, and before long he and I were sitting side by side at Mrs. Closmadene's table. The ladies had withdrawn, and we were about to follow them upstairs. Daynesborough was a frank, pleasant fellow, and scorned the affectation of concealing his happiness in the married state. In fact, he seemed to take a fancy to me, and told me that he would like me to come and see him at home.

"Then," he said, "you will cease to distrust marriage."

"I shall be most glad to come," I answered, "more especially as I want a talk with you."

"Do you? About what?"

"I have a message for you."

"You have a message for me, Mr. Jason? Forgive me, but from whom?"

I leaned over toward him, and whispered, "The Princess Ferdinand of Glottenberg."

The man turned as white as a sheet, and, gripping my hand, said under his breath:

"Hush! Surely you—you haven't—she hasn't sent it?"

"Yes, she has," said I.

"Good God! After seven years!"

General Closmadene rose from his chair. Daynesborough drank off a very large "white-wash," and added:

"Come to dinner to-morrow—eight o'clock. We shall be alone; and, for Heaven's sake, say nothing."

I said nothing, and I went to dinner, carrying the ruby ring in my breast-pocket. But I began to wonder whether the little princess was quite as childlike as she seemed.

Lady Daynesborough dined with us. She was a tall, slender girl; very handsome, and, to judge from her appearance, not wanting in resolution and character. She was obviously devoted to her husband, and he treated her with an affectionate deference that seemed to me almost overdone. It was like the manner of a man who is remorseful for having wounded someone he loves.

When she left us, he returned to the table, and, with a weary sigh, said:

"Now, Mr. Jason, I am ready."

"My task is a very short one," said I. "I have no message except to convey to you the princess' best wishes for your happiness on your marriage, of which she has recently heard, and to give you the ring. Here it is."

"Have women no mercy?" groaned he.

"I beg your pardon?" said I, rather startled.

"She waits seven years—seven years without a word or a sign—and then sends it! And why?"

"Because you're married."

"Exactly. Isn't it—devilish?"

"Not at all. It's strictly correct. She said herself that your wife was the proper person to have the ring now."

He looked at me with a bitter smile.

"My dear Jason," he said, "I have been flattering your acumen at the expense of your morality. I thought you knew what this meant."

"No more than what the princess told me."

"No, of course not, or you would not have brought it. When we parted, I gave her the ring, and she made me promise, on my honor as a gentleman, to come to her the moment she sent the ring—to leave everything and come to her, and take her away. And I promised."

"And she has never sent till now?"

"I never married till now," he said bitterly. "What's the matter with her?"

"Nothing that I know of."

He rose, went to a writing table, and came back with a fat paper book—a Continental Bradshaw.

"You're not going?" I exclaimed.

"Oh, yes! I promised."

"You promised something to your wife too, didn't you?"

"I can't argue it. I must go and see what she wants. I—I hope she'll let me come back."

I tried to dissuade him. I know I told him he was a fool; I think I told him he was a scoundrel. I was not sure of the second, but I thought it wisest to pretend that I was.

"I hope it will be all right," he said, again and again; "but, right or wrong, I must go."

I took an immediate resolution.

"I suppose you'll go by the eleven-o'clock train to Paris to-morrow?"

"Yes," he said.

"Well, you're wrong. Good-night."

At twelve o'clock the next day I called in Curzon Street, and sent in my card to Lady Daynesborough.

She saw me at once. I expect that she fancied I had something to do with her husband's sudden departure. She was looking pale and dispirited, and I rather thought she had been crying. Her husband, it appeared, had told her that he had to go to Paris on business, and would be back in three days.

"He didn't tell you what it was?"

"No. Some public affairs, I understood."

"Lady Daynesborough," said I, "you hardly know me, but my name tells you I am a gentleman."

She looked at me in surprise.

"Why, of course, Mr. Jason. But what has that to do——"

"I can't explain. But, if you are wise, you will come with me to Paris."

"Go with you to Paris! Oh! is he in danger?"

"In danger of making a fool of himself. Now, I'll say nothing more. Will you come?"

"It will look very strange."

"Very."

"In fact—most unusual."

"Most."

"Won't there be a—a—scandal, if——"

"Sure to be. Will you come?"

"You must have a reason," she said. "I will come."

We started that evening, nine hours after My Lord, going separately to the station, and meeting on the boat. All through the journey she scarcely spoke a word. When we were nearing Paris, she asked:

"Do you know where he is?"

"No; but I can trace him," I replied.

So I could. I bought a paper, and found that Prince and Princess Ferdinand had, the day before, proceeded from Paris *en route* for Glottenberg. Of course Daynesborough had followed them.

"We must go on," I said.

"Why?"

"Because your husband has gone on."

She obeyed me like a lamb; but there was a look about her pretty mouth that made me doubt if Daynesborough would find her like a lamb.

We went to the principal hotel in Glottenberg. I introduced Lady Daynesborough as my sister, Miss Jacynth Jason, and stated that she was in weak health, and would keep her room for the present. Then I sallied forth, intent on discovering Dumergue; he would be able to post me up in the state of affairs.

On my way, I met the king taking his daily drive. He was a dour, sour-looking, pasty-faced creature, and I quite understood that he would fail to appreciate many of my prince's characteristics. A priest sat by him, and a bystander told me it was the king's confessor (the Glottenberg family are all of the old church), and added that the king's confessor was no mean power in the state. I asked him where M. Dumergue was lodged, and he directed me to Prince Ferdinand's palace, which stood in a pleasant park in the suburbs of the town.

I found Dumergue in a melancholy condition, though he professed to be much cheered by the sight of me.

"My dear fellow," he said, "you, if anybody, can get us out of this."

"I never knew such people," said I. "What's up now?"

"There has been a—an explosion. Did you ever hear of Daynesborough?"

I said no, and Dumergue told me of the princess' former *penchant* for him.

"Well?" said I.

"Well, she's invited him here, and he's now in the palace. You may imagine the prince's feelings."

"I suppose the prince can turn him out?"

Dumergue shook his head dolefully.

"She holds the trumps," he answered. "Jason, she's a clever woman. We thought we had hoodwinked her. When Daynesborough turned up, looking, I'm bound to say, very sheepish, the prince was really quite annoyed. He told the princess that she must send him away. She refused flatly. 'Then I shall consult my brother,' says the prince. 'I shall consult the king too,' said the princess. 'It's indecent,' said he. 'It's not as bad as taking my ladies to masked balls in disguise,' she answered. 'Oh, you think you imposed on me—you and that clumsy young animal (forgive me, my dear fellow), Jason. I am not an idiot. I knew all the time. And now the king will know too—unless Lord Daynesborough stays just as long as I like.'"

"Confound her!" said I.

"There it is," he went on. "The prince is furious, the princess triumphant, and Daynesborough in possession."

"What does he mean to do?"

He shrugged his shoulders.

"Who can tell? She's a little devil. Fancy pretending to be deceived, and then turning on us like this! You should have heard her describe you, my boy!" and Dumergue chuckled in sad pleasure.

I object to being ridiculed, especially by women. I determined to take a hand in the game. I wondered if they knew that Daynesborough was married.

"I suppose this young Daynesborough enjoys himself?"

"Well, he ought to. He's got nothing to lose; but he seems a melancholy, glum creature. I think he must be one of the king's kidney."

"Or married, perhaps?" I suggested airily.

"Oh, no! She wouldn't have him here, if he were married."

I saw that Dumergue did not yet appreciate the princess in whose household he had the honor to serve.

"She won't compromise herself, I suppose?"

"Not she!" he replied regretfully. "She may compromise the prince."

I rebuked him for his cynicism, and promised to consider and let him know if anything occurred to me. My hope lay in Daynesborough. I could see that he was *galant malgré lui*, and I thought I could persuade him that he had done all that his mistaken promise fairly entailed on him; or, if I could not convince him, I had a suspicion that his wife might, could, and would, in a very peremptory fashion, if I brought about an encounter between them. I was full of eagerness, for, apart from my zeal in the cause of morality and domestic happiness, I did not approve of being called a clumsy young animal. It was neither true nor witty; and surely abuse ought to be one or the other, if it is to be distinguished from mere vulgar scurrility.

I have been told, by those who know the place, that Glottenberg is not, as a rule, a very exciting residence. But for the next four-and-twenty hours I, at least, had no reason to grumble at a lack of incidents.

The play began, if I may so express myself, by the princess sending for the doctor. The doctor, having heard from the princess what she wanted to do, told her what she ought to do; of course I speak from conjecture. He prescribed a visit to her country villa for a week or two, plenty of fresh air, complete repose, and freedom from worry. Dumergue told me that the princess considered that the terms of this prescription entailed a temporary separation from her husband, and that the prince had agreed to remain in Glottenberg. The princess started for her villa at twelve o'clock on Wednesday morning. The distance was but fifteen miles, and she traveled by road in her own carriage, although the main line of railway from Glottenberg to Paris passed within two miles of her destination.

At one o'clock Lord Daynesborough was received by Prince Ferdinand, having requested an interview for the purpose of taking his leave, as he left for Paris by the five o'clock train. Everybody knew that the prince and Daynesborough were not on cordial terms; but this fact hardly explained Daynesborough's extreme embarrassment and obvious discomfort during the brief conversation. Dumergue escorted him from the prince's presence, and said that he was shaking like an aspen-leaf or an ill-made blanc-mange.

At three o'clock I went to the hotel, and had an interview with Lady Daynesborough. I then returned to the palace, and made a communication to the prince. The prince was distinctly perturbed.

"I never thought she would go so far," he said. "It's not that she cares twopence about Daynesborough."

"To what, then, sir, do you attribute——"

"Temper! all temper, Mr. Jason! She is angry about that wretched ball, and she wants to anger me."

"Her Royal Highness is, however, giving a handle to her enemies," I ventured to suggest.

"She must come back to-night," said he. "I won't be made to look like a fool."

"My plan will, I hope, dispose of Lord Daynesborough. If so, Your Royal Highness might join the princess."

"I shan't do anything of the sort. I shall have her brought back."

Apparently there was a reserve of resolution latent somewhere in this indolent gentleman.

"Will you go yourself, sir?"

"No. You must do it."

"I, sir? Surely, M. Dumergue——"

"Dumergue's afraid of her. Will you bring her back?"

"Supposing she won't come?"

"I didn't request you to ask her to come. I requested you to bring her."

I looked at him inquiringly. He inhaled a mouthful of smoke, and added, with a nod:

"Yes, if necessary."

"Will Your Royal Highness hold me harmless from the king—or the law."

"No. I can't. Will you do it?"

"With pleasure, sir."

At ten minutes to five, Lady Daynesborough, heavily veiled, and I drove up to the station in a hired cab, and hid ourselves in the third-class waiting room. At five minutes to five, Lord Daynesborough arrived. He wore a scarf up to his nose, and a cap down to his eyes, and walked to the station, unattended and without luggage. He got into a second-class smoking carriage—one of the long compartments divided into separate boxes by intervening partitions reaching within a yard of the roof, a gang-way running down the middle. On seeing him enter, I caught the guard, gave him twenty marks, and told him to admit no one except myself and my companion into that carriage. Then I hauled Lady Daynesborough in, and we sat down at the opposite end to that occupied by her husband.

The train started. It was only five-and-twenty minutes' run to the station for the princess' villa. There was no time to lose.

"Are you ready?" I whispered.

"Yes," she answered, her voice trembling a little.

We rose, walked along, and sat down opposite to Lord Daynesborough. He was looking out of the window, although it was dark, and did not turn.

"Lord Daynesborough," said I, "you have forgotten your ticket." And I held out a through ticket to Paris.

He started as if he had been shot.

"Who the devil——" he began. "Jason!"

"Yes," said I. "Here's your ticket."

"I thought you were in England," he gasped.

"No, I am here."

"Spying on my actions?"

"Acquainted with them."

"I'll have no interference, sir. If you know me, you will kindly be silent, and leave me to myself."

Time was passing.

"You are going to Paris with this lady," said I.

"You're insolent, sir—you and your——"

"Don't say what you'll regret. She's your wife."

Well, of course he was very much in the wrong, and looked uncommonly ridiculous to boot. Still, the way he collapsed was rather craven. I withdrew for five minutes. Then I returned, and held out the ticket again. He took it.

"If you will leave us for five minutes, Lady Daynesborough?"

She went into the next box. Then I said:

"Now, we've only ten minutes. We're going to change clothes. Be quick."

I took off my coat.

"By God, I'll not stand this!"

And he rose.

In a moment I had him by the collar, and was presenting a pistol at his head.

"No nonsense!" I whispered. "Off with them!"

He might have known I would not shoot him in his wife's presence; but I could and would have undressed him with my own hands. Perhaps he guessed this.

"Let me go," he muttered.

I released him, and he took off his coat.

The train began to slacken speed. I called to Lady Daynesborough, who rejoined us.

"You have fulfilled your promise," said I to the young man. "And," I added, turning to her, "I have fulfilled mine. Good-night!"

I opened the door, and jumped out as we entered the station. I stood waiting till the train started again, but Lord Daynesborough remained in his place. I wonder what passed on that journey. She was a plucky girl, and I can only trust she gave him what he deserved. At any rate, he never, so far as I heard, ran away again.

I asked my way to the villa, and reached it after half an hour's walking. I did not go in by the lodge gates, but climbed the palings, and reached the door by way of the shrubberies. I knocked softly. A man opened the door instantly. He must have been waiting.

"Is it Milord?" he said in French.

"Yes," I answered, entering rapidly.

"You are expected, Milord."

I did not know his voice, and it was dark in the passage.

"I am wet," I said. "Take me to a fire."

"There is one in the pantry," he answered, leading the way.

We reached the pantry, and he turned to light the gas.

Looking at me in the full blaze, he started back, then scrutinized me closely, then exclaimed:

"What? You are not——"

"Oh, yes, I am! I am Lord Daynesborough."

"It's a lie. You are a robber—a——"

"I am Lord Daynesborough—Lord Daynesborough—Lord Daynesborough."

At each repetition I advanced a step nearer; at the last I produced my trusty pistol, at the same time holding out a bank-note in the other hand.

He took the note.

"You will stay here," I said, "for the next two hours. You will not come out, whatever happens. Is there anyone else in the house?"

"One maid, Milord, and a man in the stables."

"Where is the maid?"

"In the kitchen."

"Is the man within hearing?"

"No."

"Good! Is the princess upstairs?"

"She is, Milord."

I made him direct me to the room, and left him. I thought I would neglect the maid, and go straight to work. I went up to the door to which I had been directed, and knocked.

"Come in!" said the gentle, childlike voice.

I went in. The princess was lying on a sofa by the fire, reading a paper-covered book. She turned her head with a careless glance.

"Ah, you have come! Well, I almost hoped you would be afraid. I really don't want you."

This reception would probably have annoyed Lord Daynesborough.

"Why should I be afraid?" I asked, mimicking Daynesborough's voice as well as I could.

Meanwhile I quietly locked the door.

"Why, because of your wife. I know you tremble before her."

I advanced to the sofa.

"I have no wife," I said; "and, seeing what I do, I thank God for it."

She leaped up with a scream, loud and shrill.

A door opposite me opened, and a girl rushing in, crying:

"Madame!"

"Go back!" I said. "Go back!"

She paused, looking bewildered. I walked quickly up to her.

"Go back and keep quiet;" and, taking her by the shoulders, I pushed her back into the next room.

The princess rushed to the other door, and, on finding it locked, screamed again.

"Nobody," I remarked, "should embark on these things who has not good nerves."

She recognized me now. Her fright had been purely physical—I suppose she thought I was a burglar. When she knew me, she came forward in a dignified way, sat down on the sofa, and said:

"Explain your conduct, sir, if you are in a condition to do so."

"I am sober, madame," said I; "and I have two messages for you."

"You present yourself in a strange way. Pray be brief," and she glanced anxiously at the clock.

"Time does not press, madame," said I. "Nobody will come."

"Nobody will——— What do you mean? I expect nobody."

"Precisely, madame—and nobody will come."

Her ivory fan broke between her fingers with a sharp click.

"What do you want?" she said.

"To deliver my messages."

"Well?"

"First, Lord Daynesborough offers his apologies for being compelled to leave for Paris without tendering his farewell."

She turned very red, and then very white. But she restrained herself.

"And the other?"

"His Royal Highness requests that you will avail yourself of my escort for an immediate return to Glottenberg."

"And his reasons?"

"Oh, madame, as if I should inquire them!"

"You are merely insolent, sir. I shall not go to-night."

"His Royal Highness was very urgent."

She looked at me for a moment.

"Why had Lord Daynesborough to leave so suddenly?" she asked suspiciously.

"His wife wished it."

"Did she know where he was?"

"Apparently. She followed him to Glottenberg. She arrived there yesterday."

"Now I see—now I understand! I had to deal with a traitor."

"You must bestow trust, if you desire not to be deceived, madame. You dared to use me as a go-between."

"You had had practice in the trade."

The princess had a turn for repartee. I could not have set her right without quite an argument. I evaded the point.

"And yet Your Royal Highness thought me a clumsy animal!"

"Oh," she said, with a slight laugh, "it's wounded *amour propre*, is it? Come, Mr. Jason, I apologize. You are all that is brilliant and delightful—and English."

"Your Royal Highness is too good."

"And now, Mr. Jason, your device being accomplished, I suppose I may bid you good-night?"

"I regret, madame, that I must press the prince's request on your notice."

She sighed her usual impatient, petulant little sigh.

"Oh, you are tiresome! Pray go!"

"I cannot go without you, madame."

"I am not going—and my establishment does not admit of my entertaining gentlemen," she said, with smiling effrontery.

"Your Royal Highness refuses to allow me to attend you to Glottenberg?"

"I order you to leave this room."

"Finally refuses?"

"Go."

"Then I must add that I am commissioned, if necessary, to convey your Royal Highness to Glottenberg."

"To convey me?"

I bowed.

"You dare to threaten me?"

"I follow my instructions. Will you come, madame, or——"

"Well?"

"Will you be taken?"

I was not surprised at her vexation. Dumergue had, in his haste, called her "a little devil." She looked it then.

"You mean," she asked slowly, "that you will use force?"

I bowed.

"Then I yield," she said, after a pause.

I called the maid, and told her to order the carriage in five minutes. The silence was unbroken till it came round. The princess went into her room, and returned in cloak and hat, carrying a large muff. She was smiling.

"Ah, Mr. Jason, what can a woman do, against men? I am ready. We will go alone. The servants can follow."

I handed her into the coach, ordering the coachman to drive fast. He was the only man with us, and we were alone inside.

I began, perhaps stupidly, to apologize for my peremptory conduct. The princess smiled amiably.

"I like a man of resolution," she said, edging, I thought, a trifle nearer me, her hands nestling in her muff.

Apparently she was going to try the effect of amiability. I was prepared for this. She would not tempt me in that way.

"Your Royal Highness is most forgiving."

"Oh, that is my way," she answered, with the kindest possible glance, and she came nearer still.

"You are a most generous foe."

She turned to me with a dazzling smile.

"Don't say foe," she said, with a pretty lingering on the last word. And as she said it, I felt a knife driven hard into my ribs, and the muff dropped to the ground.

"God in heaven!" I cried.

The princess flung herself into the corner of the carriage.

"Ha—ha—ha! Ha—ha—ha!" she laughed, merrily, musically, fiendishly.

I tried to clutch her; I believe I should have killed her, I was half mad. But the blood was oozing fast from the wound—only the knife itself held my life in. Things danced before my eyes, and my hands fell on my lap.

The carriage stopped, the door opened, and the coachman appeared. It was all like a dream to me.

"Take his feet," said the princess. The man obeyed, and between them they lifted, or, rather, hauled and pushed, me out of the carriage, and laid me by the roadside. I was almost in a faint, and the last thing I was conscious of was a pretty, mocking mouth, which said:

"Won't you escort me, Mr. Jason?"—and then added to the coachman, "To Glottenberg—quick!"

I did not die. I was picked up by some good folk, and well tended. Dumergue arrived and looked after me, and in a couple of weeks I was on my legs.

"Now for Glottenberg!" said I.

Dumergue shook his head.

"You won't be admitted to the town."

"Not admitted!"

"No. They have made it up—for the time. There must be no scandal. Come, Jason; surely you see that?"

"She tried to murder me."

"Oh, quite, quite!" said he. "But you can't prosecute her."

"And I am to be turned adrift by the prince?"

"What use would it be to return? No doubt you annoyed her very much."

"I wish you had undertaken the job."

"I know her. I should have ridden outside."

"It is, then, the prince's wish that I should not return?"

"Yes. But he charges me to say that he will never forget your friendly services."

I was disgusted. But I would force myself on no man.

"Then I'll go home."

"That will be much best," he answered, with revolting alacrity.

"I say, Dumergue, what does the princess say about me?"

"She laughs every time your name is mentioned, and——"

"The devil take her!"

"She says you may keep the knife!"

I have it still, a little tortoise-shell-handled thing, with a sharp—a very sharp—point. On the blade is engraved, in German letters, "Sophia." It is a pretty toy, and in its delicacy, its tininess, its elegance, its seeming harmlessness, and its very sharp point, it reminds me much of Princess Ferdinand of Glottenberg.

A TRAGEDY IN OUTLINE.

I.

Dear Mr. Brown: *   *   *   *Yours sincerely,M. Robinson.

II.

My Dear Mr. Brown: * * * *Always yours very sincerely, Minnie Robinson.

III.

My Dear Jack (!): * * * *Yours always, Minnie Robinson.

IV.

My Dearest Jack: * * * *Yours, Minnie.

V.

My Darling Jack: * * * *Lovingly, your Min.

VI.

My Dearest Jack: * * * *Lovingly, Minnie.

VII.

My Dear Jack: * * * *With love, Yours, Minnie.

VIII.

Dear Jack: * * * *Ever yours, Minnie Robinson.

IX.

My Dear Mr. Brown: * * * *Your sincere friend, Minnie Robinson.

X.

Dear Mr. Brown: * * * *Yours sincerely, M. Robinson.

XI.

Silence.

A MALAPROPOS PARENT.

YOUNG Mr. Pippitt had a father somewhere in America. Everyone who knew young Mr. Pippitt knew that; for he had often spoken of his father, of the fortune he was making, and of the liberal presents he sent home. Then came a time when young Mr. Pippitt said less about his father and less about the presents. Thus it was that people had almost forgotten the existence of old Mr. Pippitt, when it was recalled to their memories in a very startling and tragical way. Old Mr. Pippitt had landed in England and was on his way to London, when he was killed in a great railway disaster. His name, discovered from a letter in his pocket, was published; and young Mr. Pippitt flew to the scene. The body was not mangled or disfigured, and after one moment of extreme agitation the bereaved son informed the official who had led him to where the dead man lay that it was indeed his father. His evidence before the coroner put the matter beyond doubt. Mr. Pippitt buried his father, assumed deep mourning, and wrote to the company's solicitors. Repugnant as it was to him to appear to make money out of the unhappy occurrence, the loss of a rich and liberal parent was a matter which no struggling young man could, in justice to himself, submit to without compensation.

Railway companies, having an extensive experience of humanity, are prone to skepticism; and very many inquiries were made as to the life, doings, profession, and profits of old Mr. Pippitt, and especially as to his alleged remittances to his son. That gentleman stood the fire of questions very successfully; he had letters from his father up to within six months of the accident, and he proved the receipt of very considerable yearly sums, in each of the four years during which his father had been absent. In face of this evidence, the matter in issue reduced itself to a difference of opinion between the company and young Mr. Pippitt: first, as to the probability of old Mr. Pippitt continuing to make money; secondly, as to the probability of his continuing to share what he made with his son. More concretely still, the company, without prejudice, offered two thousand pounds, and Mr. Pippitt, without prejudice, asked seven thousand; whereupon the case was entered for trial.

Mr. Naylor, the company's counsel, declared that young Mr. Pippitt was one of the best witnesses he had ever seen. His demeanor was excellent, his facts irrefragable, his memory neither unnaturally bad nor suspiciously good. The last letter he produced from his father inclosed a draft for three hundred pounds, and announced the writer's return on a business visit by the next mail but one. By that mail, a gentleman of the name of Pippitt had crossed the ocean, and had, presumably, taken the train on landing, and met his death in the accident. Mr. Naylor felt his case was so bad that he almost charged young Mr. Pippitt with direct perjury, and twisted up a note to Mr. Budge, who was on the other side, offering four thousand pounds and costs. Mr. Budge answered that he must consult his client, and that he would wait till the end of the plaintiff's evidence. Mr. Naylor nodded, and redoubled his insinuations of an unscrupulous conspiracy.

Mr. Budge rose to re-examine with a smile on his face. Mr. Pippitt said he had no reason to anticipate a falling-off in his father's business; it was well established: nor in his father's liberality; his father had always led him to suppose that he would provide for him. Yes, there was a strong—yes, a very strong, affection between them. Here Mr. Pippitt's voice faltered; the judge nodded sympathetically; and the foreman of the jury wrote "£5,000?" on a slip of paper and passed it round the box.

That artistic falter produced another effect also. The gangways of the court were crowded with the usual throng of idle folk, assembled to hear Mr. Naylor's cross-examination; and as the plaintiff bore witness to the bonds of love which bound him to his father there came from the recesses of the crowd a voice, which said:

"That there is! Let me through! Who's saying my boy doesn't love his old father?"

The group of people parted; and an elderly man came to the front, advancing in an uncertain, apologetic manner.

"Silence! silence!" cried the usher, a world of pained indignation in his accents.

"You mustn't disturb the court, sir!" thundered the judge.

"I came to speak a word for Joe. I was passing, and dropped in, and, seeing Joe, I made bold to speak. He's been a good son, has Joe."

The judge looked appealingly at counsel.

"Who is Joe, and who is this person?" And getting no answer, he turned to the plaintiff. Young Mr. Pippitt met his eye with an uneasy smile.

"I haven't the least idea, my lord," he said.

The judge looked at the writ.

"Your name is Joseph?" he asked.

"No, it—yes—that is, certainly, my lord."

"You don't seem very sure, sir," remarked the judge; and he added, addressing the intruder, "Who are you, sir?"

The old man seemed in a nervous and broken-down condition; but he stammered out, "He's my son, my son, my lord."

"It's a lie," cried young Mr. Pippitt.

"Hold your tongue till you're asked to speak," said his lordship snappishly. "I want to hear what this man has to say."

The old man had much to say: much of young Mr. Pippitt's virtue, industry, and much of his own fortunes, misfortunes, and wrongs. He usurped the functions of both lawyer and witness, and all the court listened to him.

"I'm glad to be here, gentlemen," he said—"glad to be here. I thought I was never going to get out of that cell they put me in, not for long years. But here I am, Joe, thank God!"

"Who put you in a cell?" asked the judge.

"I'm telling you as fast as I can," answered the old man petulantly. "I'd just written to Joe to send him a bit of money and tell him to look out for me, when they brought a charge of fraud against me—against me, a respectable merchant. And I was tried: tried and found guilty—unjustly, my lord—and sentenced to five years. To think of it! They didn't know me out in Louisiana; no east-coast jury would have convicted."

"Why didn't they know you?"

"I wasn't going to have my name known. I called myself Brown; and they convicted me—as I wrote to you, Joe—for five years. But the Governor did his duty. He was a white man, the Governor. He let me out."

"Why?" asked the judge curiously.

"Was a white man to get five years for besting a nigger?" demanded the old man, with his first approach to vigor. "Not if the Governor knew it! Oh, he was a white man. So here I am, Joe—here I am, thank God!"

The judge leaned forward and asked, "Have you any letters from the man you say is your son?"

The old man pulled a dirty letter out of his pocket, and handed it up with a bewildered look.

Young Mr. Pippitt still looked on with his fixed smile, while the judge read:

"DEAR FATHER:

"It's a bad job that you're nabbed. Five years is no joke. Why were you such a fool? You were right about the name. Keep it quite dark, for God's sake! I'll see what I can do.

"Yours,
"J. P.

"Received your last all right."

"Is that your handwriting?" the judge asked of the plaintiff; but young Mr. Pippitt swayed to and fro and fell in a faint in the witness-box. The judge turned to Mr. Budge.

"Do you desire," he asked, "that this man should be sworn, and repeat his evidence on oath, so that you may cross-examine him?"

Mr. Budge looked at his inanimate client, and answered, "I do not, my lord. I shall probably have your lordship's approval in withdrawing from the case?"

While the judge directed the jury to return a verdict for the defendant, the old man had anxiously watched the usher, who was unloosing young Mr. Pippitt's neckcloth. When the plaintiff revived, the old man leaned over to Mr. Budge, and said, with a pleased smile, "Oh, he'll be all right directly, won't he? I thought I could help a bit. I have helped a bit, haven't I?"

"You have helped him to twelve months' hard labor," said Mr. Budge.

But the old man did not understand what it all meant, till one day they took him to Kensal Green, and showed him a handsome tombstone. The inscription ran:

"IN MEMORY OF JAMES PIPPITT."

The old man read and laughed.

"To think of that!" he said. "It beats everything!"

He read on with a chuckle:

"Erected by his sorrowing son, Joseph Pippitt. Born 13th December, 1821. Died 5th February, 1891. 'I shall go to him, but he shall not return to me.'"

This prophecy might or might not be true of the person interred beneath the tombstone. On its unfortunate inapplicability to his father, and on the tainting of the fountain of Louisiana justice, young Mr. Pippitt enjoyed twelve months' quiet reflection.

HOW THEY STOPPED THE "RUN."

THERE was a run on the Sandhill and District Bank. It had lasted the whole of one day, and had shown no signs of abating in the evening. If it lasted another day! Old Mr. Bradshaw wiped his brow. It had come just at the awkwardest time—just after the farmers had got their usual loans, just when securities were hard to realize; in fact, just at the moment when the bank, though in reality solvent, was emphatically not in a position in answer a long-continued demand for payment on the spot. Mr. Bradshaw groaned out all these distressing facts to his son Dick. It was, indeed, no use talking to Dick, for he took no interest in business, and had spent the day in a boat with the Flirtington girls; still, Mr. Bradshaw was bound to talk to someone.

"We shall have to put the shutters up. One day's grace would save us, I believe; we could get the money then. But if they're at us again to-morrow morning, we can't last two hours."

Dick sympathized, but had nothing to suggest, except that it would not make matters worse if he carried out his engagement to go to the circus with the Flirtington girls.

"Oh, go to h—ll with the Flirtington girls, if you like," groaned Mr. Bradshaw.

So Dick went—to the circus (the other expedition, as he observed, would keep), and enjoyed the performance very much, especially the lion-taming, which was magnificent, and so impressed Dick that he deserted his companions, went behind the scenes, and insisted on standing Signor Philippini several glasses.

"Is that big chap quite safe?" he asked admiringly.

"I can do anythink with 'im," said the signor (whose English was naturally defective); "but with anyone helse 'e's a roarer, 'e is, and no mistake."

After the performance Dick took the Flirtington girls home; then, with a thoughtful look on his face, he went and had some talk with his father, and came away, carefully placing a roll of notes in his breast pocket. Then he sought Signor Philippini's society once more. And that's all that is really known about it—if, that is, we discard the obviously fanciful statement of Fanny Flirtington that, as she was gazing at the moon about 2 A. M., she saw a heavy wagon, drawn by two horses and driven by Signor Philippini, pass along the street in the direction of the bank. She must have been wrong; for Philippini, by the evidence of his signora (whose name, notwithstanding that Philippini's morals were perfectly correct, was Mrs. Buggins), went to bed at 11.30, and snored like a pig all night.

However these things may be, this is what happened next morning. When the first of the depositors arrived at 7 A. M., they found one of the windows of the bank smashed to pieces and the shutter hanging loose. A cry went up that there had been a robbery, and one or two men began to climb in. They did not get far before a fearful roar proceeded from the neighborhood of the counter. They looked at one another, and said it would be more regular to wait for the officials. The roars continued. They sent for Mr. Bradshaw. Hardly had he arrived (accompanied by Dick, breathless and in shirt-sleeves) before the backmost rows of the now considerable crowd became agitated with a new sensation. The news spread rapidly. Frantic men ran to and fro; several ladies fainted; the circus-proprietor was sent for. A lion had escaped from the menagerie, and was supposed to be at large in the town!

"Send for Philippini!" cried the proprietor. They did so. Philippini had started early for a picnic in the country, and would not return till just before the performance in the evening. The proprietor was in despair.

"Where's the beast gone to?" he cried.

A roar from the bank answered his question.

"Well, I'm blowed if he's not in the bank!" exclaimed the proprietor.

It certainly appeared to be the fact that Atlas (that was the lion's name) had taken refuge in the bank, and was in full possession of the premises and assets. Under these circumstances there was, Mr. Bradshaw explained, a difficulty in resuming cash payments; but if his checks would be accepted—— The crowd roared almost as loud as Atlas at such an idea. Something must be done. They sent for the mayor; he repudiated liability. They sent for the fire brigade and the lifeboat crew; neither would come. They got guns, and peppered the furniture. Atlas retired behind the fireproof safe and roared worse than ever. Meanwhile the precious hours were passing. Mr. Bradshaw's money was also on its way from London. At last Dick took a noble resolution.

"I will go in at any cost," he cried, and, in spite of Fanny Flirtington's tears, he scaled the window and disappeared from view. The crowd waited to hear Atlas scrunching; but he only roared. When Dick was inside, he paused and asked in a low voice: "Is he chained?"

"Yes," answered Signor Philippini from behind the safe. "Is the Aunt Sally business over?" and he came out with a long pole in his hand. He used the pole to stir poor Atlas up when the roars became deficient in quantity and quality.

"The money ought to be here in three hours," said Dick. "Have you got the back-door key?"

Philippini reassured him. Then Dick took a wild running leap at the window; Philippini stirred up Atlas, who roared lustily. Dick escaped with his life, and landed, a breathless heap, at the mayor's feet. The mayor raised him, and said he should write to Her Majesty, and suggest that Dick would be a proper recipient of the Albert Medal, and the vicar (who had no money in the bank) indignantly asked the crowd if they could not trust a family which produced scions like that. Several people cried "Hear, hear!" and told Mr. Bradshaw that they never really meant to withdraw their deposits. Mr. Bradshaw thanked them, and looked at his watch.

At half-past three Philippini ran up; he also was breathless, and his shoes were dusty from walking in the country. At once he effected an entry, amid a scene of great excitement. A moment later he appeared at the window and cried in a terror-stricken voice:

"I can't 'old 'im! I can't 'old 'im! 'E's mad! Look out for yourselves!" and he leaped from the window.

The crowd fled in all directions, and two boys were all but run over by a cart which was being driven rapidly from the railway station to the bank.

"All right," said Dick to the signor; "bring up the wagon." And then, with great difficulty and consummate courage, the signor and Dick brought an iron cage up to the window, and drove Atlas in. The operation took more than an hour, because they had to feed Atlas and drink a bottle of champagne themselves before they set about it. So that it was six o'clock before Atlas was out, and the money was in, and the Sandhill and District Bank opened its doors for business.

"We gained just the time we needed," said Mr. Bradshaw. "It was dirt-cheap at fifty pounds!"

And Dick, although he did not get the Albert Medal, was taken into partnership, and married Fanny Flirtington. It was the only way of preventing her seeing things she was not meant to see out of the window at 2 A. M. and chattering about them in public.

A LITTLE JOKE.

A DAY or two before Easter, I was sitting in my office, finishing up some scraps of work, and ever and anon casting happy glances at my portmanteau, which stood in the corner. I was just off to spend a fortnight with my old friend Colonel Gunton, in Norfolk, and I was looking forward to seeing him again with great pleasure. We had not met for ten years, and I had never been to his place or seen any of his family. It would be delightful.

The telephone bell rang.

"Oh, confound it! I hope that's nothing to keep me!" I exclaimed; and I rose to see to it.

"Mr. Miller? Are you there?"

"Yes."

"All right. I'll come round."

A few minutes passed, and then my clerk announced, "A lady to see you, sir."

A remarkably pretty girl of about eighteen was ushered in. She stood still some way from me till the door was closed. Then she suddenly rushed toward me, fell at my feet, and exclaimed, "You will protect me, won't you?"

"My dear young lady, what in the world——"

"You're the famous Mr. Miller, aren't you? Mr. Joseph Miller, the philanthropist?"

"My name is Joseph Miller certainly."

"Ah! Then I am safe;" and she sat down in an armchair, and smiled confidingly at me.

"Madam," said I sternly, "will you have the goodness to explain to what I owe the pleasure of this visit?"

"They told me to come to you."

"Who?"

"Why, the people at the police station."

"The police station?"

"Yes, when they let me go—because it was a first offense, you know. They said you always took up cases like mine, and that if I stuck to you I should be well looked after."

It was quite true that I have taken an interest in rescuing young persons from becoming habitual criminals; but I was hardly prepared for this.

"What have you been doing?"

"Oh, nothing this time—only a bracelet."

"This time?"

"They didn't know me up here," she explained smilingly. "I've always practiced in the country. Wasn't it lucky? But really, Mr. Miller, I'm tired of it; I am indeed. The life is too exciting: the doctors say so; so I've come to you."

The case was a strange one, but I had no time to investigate it now. It wanted only half an hour to the time my train left Liverpool Street.

"What is your name?" I asked.

"Sarah Jones."

"Well, I will have your case looked into. Come and see me again; or, if you are in distress, you may write to me—at Colonel Gunton's, Beech Hill, Norfolk. I shall be staying there——"

"Going now?"

"I start in a few minutes."

"Oh, I'll come with you."

"Madam," I answered, with emphasis, "I will see you—out of the office first."

"But what am I to do? Oh, it's nonsense! I shall come. I shall say I belong to you."

I rang the bell. "Show this lady out, Thomas, at once."

She laughed, bowed, and went. Evidently a most impudent hussy. I finished my business, drove to Liverpool Street, and established myself in a first-class smoking carriage. I was alone, and settled myself for a comfortable cigar. I was rudely interrupted. Just as the train was starting, the door opened—and that odious young woman jumped in.

"There! I nearly missed you!" she said.

"I can hold no communication with you," said I severely; "you are a disgrace to your—er—sex."

"It's all right. I've wired to the colonel."

"You've wired to my friend Colonel Gunton?"

"Yes, I didn't want to surprise them. I said you would bring a friend with you. It's all right, Mr. Miller."

"I don't know who you are or what you are; but the Guntons are respectable people, and I am a respectable man, and——"

"That's no reason why you should promenade up and down, Mr. Miller. It's very uncomfortable for me."

"What is the meaning of this insolent behavior?"

"Why not be friendly? We're off now, and I must go on."

"I shall give you in charge at the next station."

"What for?"

On reflection, I supposed she had committed no criminal offense; and with a dignified air I opened my paper.

"I don't mind you smoking," she said, and took out a box of chocolates.

I was at my wits' end. Either this girl was mad or she was a dangerous and unscrupulous person. She was quite capable of making a most unpleasant and discreditable commotion on the platform at Beach Hill Station. What in the world was I to do?

"Shall we stay long at the Guntons'?" she asked.

"You, madam, will never go there."

"Oh, yes, I shall."

"Indeed you won't. I'll take care of that. The police will see to that."

"I don't care a fig for the police. I shall go and stay as long as you do. They told me to stick to you."

I became angry. Any man would have. But nothing was to be gained by losing my temper. I took out a sovereign.

"If you'll get out at the next station, I'll give you this."

She laughed merrily. "I thought you went in for personal supervision, not mere pecuniary doles," she said; "I read that in your speech at the Charity Organization meeting. No; I'm not to be bribed. I'm going to the Guntons'."

"It's absurd. It's preposterous. What will—what will Mrs. Gunton say?"

"Oh, she won't mind," answered my companion, with a confident nod. "She's used to girls like me."

"You surprise me," I retorted sarcastically; but she only laughed again. I returned to my paper.

An hour passed in silence. The train began to slacken speed as we neared the station next before Beech Hill. She looked up and said:

"Would you really rather I didn't come with you?"

I had passed a wretched hour. This girl was evidently bent on blasting my character.

"Madam," I said, "if you'll get out at this station, I'll give you a five-pound note."

"What? I heard you never gave away a farthing! They said no one could get a penny out of you."

"It is true that I disapprove of indiscriminate charity; but, under the circumstances, I——"

"Think I am a deserving object? Well, I'll take it."

With a sigh of relief, I took a note from my pocket-book, and gave it her.

"I'll pay it back soon," she said.

"Never let me see your face again."

"Apologize for me to the Guntons. Good-by."

She jumped out lightly, and I sank back, murmuring, "Thank Heaven!"

After I got rid of her my journey was peaceful and happy, and I forgot my troubles in the warm greeting my old friend Bob Gunton and his wife gave me. The girl must have lied about the telegram; at least, Bob made no reference to it. He had a fine family of boys and girls, and presented them to me with natural pride.

"That's my lot—except Addie. She's gone to see some friends; but we expect her back every minute. They keep me alive, I can tell you, Miller."

After tea, my host and hostess insisted on taking me for a stroll on the terrace. It was a beautiful evening, and I did not mind the cold. As we were talking together, I heard the rumble of wheels. An omnibus stopped at the gate.

"Ah, the 'bus," said Gunton; "it runs between here and our market-town."

I hardly heard him; for, to my horror, I saw, descending from the 'bus and opening the gate, that girl!

"Send her away!" I cried; "send her away! On my honor, Bob, as a gentleman, I know nothing about her."

"Why, what's the matter?"

"I solemnly assure Mrs. Gunton and yourself that——"

"What's the matter with the man? What's he talking about?"

"Why, Bob, that girl—that barefaced girl!"

"That girl! Why, that's my daughter Addie!"

"Your daughter?"

The little minx walked up to me with a smile, dropped a little courtesy, and said: "I knew, Mr. Miller, that it wasn't true that you would refuse to help a really deserving case. The others said you would; but I thought better of you."

And she had the effrontery, then and there, to tell her parents all about it!

I think parents are the most infatuated class of persons in the community. They laughed, and Mrs. Gunton said, "How clever of you, Addie! You must forgive her, Mr. Miller. My dear girls are so playful!"

Playful! And she never returned the five-pound note!

A GUARDIAN OF MORALITY.

MISS TABITHA GREY had not reached the age of forty-five years without acquiring an extensive and unfavorable knowledge of her sex. Men were wicked; Miss Grey admitted and deplored the fact, but it was so much in the order of nature that she had almost ceased to cavil at it. But that women should be wicked! Here Miss Grey's toleration gave out. And so many women, especially young women, and more especially pretty young women, were wicked. It was atrocious! Entertaining this general opinion, Miss Grey, as a matter of course, held Maggie Lester in the utmost detestation. The Waterfall Hotel was, in fact, hardly large enough to contain, in any comfort, Miss Grey on the one hand and on the other Maggie Lester, her brother Charles, and their friend and traveling companion. Captain Petrie. It is true that the feeling of discomfort was entirely confined to Miss Grey. The young people were very civil to her when any one of them happened to be next her at *table d'hôte*, and at other times thought nothing about her; but Miss Grey endured agonies enough for an hotelful of people. She shuddered at Maggie's striped waistcoat and white sailor's knot with its golden pin, at her brown boots, at her love of long and hard rides, at her not infrequent slang; above all, at the terms of hearty and familiar *camaraderie* on which she thought fit to conduct her acquaintance with Captain Petrie. The decorum of literature forbids that Miss Grey's inmost suspicions should be put in writing; it must suffice to say that they were very dark indeed—so dark that all the other ladies, to whom Miss Grey repeated them, could not but come to the conclusion that there must be some truth in them.

One morning, after breakfast, Miss Grey took her knitting and the Church Times and sat down in the veranda. A moment later, to her disgust, Charlie Lester and Captain Petrie came out of the breakfast room, lit their pipes, and, after a polite "Good-morning," took their seats a few yards from her. Miss Grey sniffed the tobacco-tainted air, and was about to rise and ostentatiously remove herself from the infected zone, when she heard a scrap of conversation between the two young men which entirely altered her determination. She sat still and listened with all her might.

"I wonder when Maggie will be down," said Lester; "I want to tell her."

"Oh, you're too late," said Petrie; "I've told her."

"What, have you seen her?"

"Yes. I knew she'd like to know, so I went outside her door five minutes ago and shouted what we'd heard, and she came out directly."

"Had she anything on?" inquired Lester, in an interested tone.

"No," responded Captain Petrie; "but that made no difference."

"It would to me," said Lester, with a smile.

"And to me," said the captain; "but it didn't to her. I reminded her of it, and she said that it made no odds—she wanted to hear all I knew directly. So we stood in the passage, and——"

Miss Grey had been gradually becoming more and more horrified. She had been prepared for a good deal, but this was too much. And the creature's own brother listened to it! Her knitting fell from her grasp, and the needles jangled on the tiled floor. The captain hastened to pick them up, interrupting his narrative for that purpose; but Miss Grey froze him with an awful look, and strode into the house.

Miss Grey was a woman who never allowed herself to be turned from the path of duty, however painful that path might be to others. She soon made up her mind as to what she must do, and, having come to a resolution, she laid the whole matter before an informal committee of three irreproachable and austere matrons, whom she selected from among her fellow-guests. The immediate result of their conference was, that when Maggie Lester, looking very fresh and blooming after her morning gallop, came in to luncheon and took her place at the table, no fewer than four elderly ladies put down their knives and forks, rose from their chairs, and solemnly stalked out of the room.

"Hullo! what's up?" said Charlie Lester.

But nobody knew what was up; and, to all appearance, Maggie least of all, for she cheerfully began her lunch, mere remarking to the captain, as though in continuance of a previous conversation:

"It wouldn't have been so bad if I'd had anything—even the least little bit—on, would it?"

"Ah, you ought to have put your boots on," said the captain, with a smile.

A fifth lady, sitting by, overheard these remarks, and when, after lunch, Miss Grey informed her of the startling occurrence of the morning, her testimony completed the damning chain of evidence. They made a joke of it! What could the suggestion of boots—only boots—be, except a vulgar, shameless jest? The ladies went in a body to the proprietor, and intimated that either they or the Lester party must forthwith leave the hotel. The proprietor demanded reasons; cogent, irrefragable reasons were supplied by Miss Grey and the fifth lady—reasons clothed, of course, in decorous language, but unmistakably revealing the infamous conduct of Maggie Lester.

"I assure you, ladies," exclaimed the proprietor, beads of perspiration standing on his brow, "it's the first time such a thing has ever occurred in my house."

"It must be the last," said Miss Grey firmly.

"I will act at once," declared the proprietor. "This is a respectable house, and such proceedings cannot be tolerated. Good gracious! It would endanger my license!"

"And your soul," said Miss Grey solemnly.

"I beg your pardon, miss?" said the proprietor.

"And your soul," repeated Miss Grey.

"Oh, yes, to be sure—of course, my soul, miss. As it was, I had a bother about it last year—my license, I mean, miss. I'll go to Mr. Lester at once."

The proprietor was a nervous, bashful man, and when he found himself standing before the Lesters and Captain Petrie, as they drank their after-luncheon coffee, he was much embarrassed. At last he managed to indicate that he wished to speak to Mr. Lester alone.

"Oh, nonsense!" said Charlie. "Go on. What's the matter?"

The proprietor nerved himself for the effort. After all, if these people were not ashamed for themselves, why should he blush for them? Looking sternly at Charlie, he began to formulate his accusation. He had not got far before Maggie gave a little shriek of amazement; and the captain, jumping up, seized him by the collar, and exclaimed:

"What do you mean, you little rascal? What's this scandalous nonsense you've got hold of?" and the captain shook his host severely.

"I am not to be bullied, sir," said the proprietor stoutly. "I have excellent authority for what I say, and——"

"Whose authority?"

The proprietor vouched Miss Grey and the fifth lady.

"We must look into this," said the captain.

Maggie, who was blushing severely, but was not without a secret tendency to convulsive laughter, was prevailed upon to accompany them, and the four proceeded to the drawing room, where the Inquisition sat enthroned on the sofa, Miss Grey presiding. Miss Grey rose with a gesture of horror.

"Not gone yet?" she exclaimed.

"No, ma'am," said the captain; "we want to hear your story first."

"Have you no shame?" demanded Miss Grey of Maggie.

"Never mind that, ma'am," said the captain; "let's have the story first."

Miss Grey cast an appealing glance at the ceiling, and began: "With my own ears I heard it. Mrs. Britson Mrs. Britson was the fifth la will confirm what I say. With my own ears I heard Captain Petrie relate to Mr. Lester—to this person's brother—that he had had an interview with this person when this person was entirely——" Miss Grey paused for a moment, gathered her courage, and added in an awestruck whisper, "disrobed."

A shudder ran through the audience. The culprits' faces expressed real or simulated astonishment.

"If I must put it plainly," pursued Miss Grey—and at this several ladies opened their fans and held them before their faces—"Captain Petrie said that Miss Lester—that person—had nothing on, and that when he reminded her of it she stated that the circumstance was immaterial. Subsequently, at luncheon, the young woman herself admitted the fact in the hearing of Mrs. Britson. If that is not enough——"

It apparently was enough, for Charlie Lester threw himself into an armchair with a wild shriek of laughter. Maggie's slight figure shook convulsively as she hid her face in her handkerchief, and Captain Petrie, after a moment's blank amazement, cried out:

"By Jove! I've got it. Oh! this beats anything!" And he joined in with a loud guffaw.

"Is that the way you treat such a—an abominable——" began Miss Grey austerely.

"Oh, stop! for Heaven's sake stop!" exclaimed the captain; "you'll be the death of me, you really will!"

Silence followed for a moment, and the captain, conquering his mirth, went on: "I don't know if any of you ladies go in for horse-racing. Probably not; I'm sure Miss Grey doesn't. Well, this morning I heard that a horse of mine which is running in a race to-day had done an exceptionally and quite unexpectedly good trial—I mean, had proved a far faster runner than we had supposed. In fact, there was little doubt that he would win the race. Sometimes, ladies, I am wicked enough to bet. Occasionally Charlie Lester is equally wicked. Now and then Miss Lester yields to that vice. Well, as you know, we are far from a telegraph here; and we were much annoyed, Charlie and I, that we could not take advantage of our fresh information to bet on the horse—to put something on, as we say. Miss Lester regretted also, when I told her the news, that she had nothing on—the horse. Do you begin to understand, ladies?"

The ladies glanced at one another in some confusion. Miss Grey looked angry and suspicious.

"And the boots?" she said.

"To put your boots on a horse," explained the captain politely, "is a slang expression for betting your entire available fortune on his success. Another expression is to put your shirt——"

"Sir!" said Miss Grey.

But Miss Grey's sway was ended. Maggie burst into a fresh fit of laughter, and, after a moment's pause the whole company followed suit. Miss Grey turned and left the room. The next day she left the hotel; she could not face her victorious foes. Captain Petrie insisted on handing her into the omnibus, saying as he did so, "Be easy, my dear madam. In future it shall be my care to see that Miss Lester has something on."

NOT A BAD DEAL.

THE little volume of verses entitled, "To Lalage," made quite a stir in the literary world. One critic of note said that it was instinct with classic grace; another that it was informed by the true spirit of Hellas; a third that it had a whiff of Hymettus; a fourth that it was hardly suitable for family reading; and on the strength of all this laudation, "To Lalage" was a success, and several copies were *bonâ fide* sold to complete strangers. Imagine, then, the bitterness of heart with which Adrian Pottles, the gifted author, saw himself compelled to maintain strict anonymity, and to conceal from a world thirsting to know him that he was the "A. P." whose initials appeared in Old English letters on the title-page. Yet he did not hesitate; for he knew that if his uncle, Mr. Thomas Pottles, of Clapham Common, discovered that he wrote not only verses, which was bad, but amatory verses, which was atrocious, his means of present livelihood and prospects of future affluence would vanish into thin air. For Mr. Pottles was a man of strict views; and, whether one regarded this world or the next, there could be no question that a bank clerk of Evangelical connections committed a grave fault in writing love poems. So poor Adrian had to make up his mind to remain unknown, and to hold his tongue even when he heard that another man had been claiming the authorship of "To Lalage." Luckily, perhaps, he failed to find out who this miscreant was, or probably his indignation would have overcome his prudence, and he would at any cost have claimed his own.

The secret was well kept; and Adrian received the usual check at Christmas-time, and with it the usual invitation to spend the festive season with his uncle, and to bring with him his young friend Peter Allison, to whom old Mr. Pottles had taken a great fancy. Peter was a man of many engagements, but, sought after as he was and proclaimed himself to be, he remembered the good cheer at Mr. Pottles', and accepted the invitation. They went down together; Adrian bewailing his hard fortune and denouncing the impostor; Peter warmly sympathizing, but counseling continued silence and prudence.

"Ah, if I could only claim it!" cried Adrian, opening his Gladstone bag and gazing fondly at half a dozen neat, clean copies of "To Lalage." "I should be the lion of the season, Peter."

Peter smiled and shook his head. "A fortune is better than fame, Adrian," said he.

For a day or two all went well at Clapham. The old gentleman was in the best of tempers, and the two young men did their best to keep him in it, indorsing all his views as to the lax morality and disgraceful tone which pervaded modern literature and modern society; and when they had done their duty in this way they rewarded themselves by going in next door and having tea with Dora Chatterton, a young lady whom they both thought charming. Indeed, Adrian thought her so charming that, after a short acquaintance, he sent her a copy of "To Lalage"—with the author's kind regards. Now, Miss Dora Chatterton adored genius. She had thought both Adrian and Peter very pleasant young men; she had perceived that they both thought her a very pleasant young woman; and she had been rather puzzled to know which of them she would, in a certain event, make up her mind to prefer. "To Lalage" settled the question. It was the gifted author, A. P., who deserved her love; and A. P. obviously stood, not for Peter Allison, but for Adrian Pottles.

The very next morning she called early at Mr. Pottles'. She found him alone; the boys, he explained, had gone for a walk. Dora was disappointed; but, failing the author himself, she was content to pour her praises into the ears of an appreciative and proud uncle. She did so, expressing immense admiration for Adrian's modesty in not having told Mr. Pottles of his achievement.

"Humph!" said Mr. Pottles. "Let me see these—er—things."

The effect of "To Lalage" on Mr. Pottles was surprising, and particularly so to Dora. In less than ten minutes she found herself being shown the door, and intrusted with a letter to her mother in which Mr. Pottles stated that she had been reading wicked books, and ought, in his opinion, to be sent to her own room for an indefinite period.

"And I shall know if you don't give it her," said Mr. Pottles viciously.

Thus it happened that Adrian and Peter, as they were returning, met poor Dora on the steps with this horrid note in one hand and her pocket-handkerchief in the other—for Mrs. Chatterton shared Mr. Pottles' views, and Dora did not enjoy having to deliver the note. They were just hastening up to speak to her, when Mr. Pottles himself appeared on the steps, holding out "To Lalage" in his hand. Adrian grasped the situation.

"For Heaven's sake, Peter," he whispered, "say you wrote the beastly thing; I'm ruined if you don't."

"Eh? But he'll kick me out."

"I'll stand a pony."

"Two," said Peter firmly.

"Well, two; but be quick."

Then Peter spoke up like a man, and accepted the blame of "To Lalage."

"But your initials aren't A. P.," objected Mr. Pottles.

"To avoid suspicion, I reversed the order; mine are P. A."

"James," said Mr. Pottles to the footman, "pack Mr. Allison's bag."

But Dora gave Peter the kindest and most admiring glance as she murmured softly to Adrian, "They're lovely! Oh, don't you wish you could write verses, Mr. Pottles?"

Adrian started. He had not bargained for this; but Peter had overheard, and interposed:

"I am more than consoled by your approval, Miss Chatterton."

Mr. Pottles called to Adrian, and he had to go in, leaving Dora and Peter in close conversation, and to assure his uncle solemnly that he had been entirely disappointed and deceived in Peter, and, worse still, in Dora, and that he never wished to see either of them again. Mr. Pottles shook him by the hand and forgave him.

Adrian passed a wretched week. In several newspapers he saw it openly stated that Peter now admitted he was the author of "To Lalage." Peter wrote that the fifty pounds were most convenient, and that he had had a most charming letter from Dora, and that all the literary world was paying him most flattering attentions. Adrian ground his teeth, but he had to write back, thanking Peter for all his kindness.

Meanwhile Mr. Pottles grew restless. Every paper he took up was full of the praises of "To Lalage." The author was becoming famous, and Mr. Pottles began to doubt whether he had done well to drive him forth with contumely.

"Adrian," he said suddenly one morning, "I don't know that I did justice to young Allison. I shall have another look at that book. I shall order it at Smith's."

"I—I happen to have a copy," said Adrian timidly.

"Get it," said Mr. Pottles. Mr. Pottles read it—first with a deep frown, then with a judicial air, then with a smile, lastly with a chuckle.

"Ask him to dinner," he said. "Oh, and, Adrian, we'll have the Chattertons. I wish you could do something to get your name up, my boy."

"You like it, uncle?"

"Yes, and I like the manly way he owned to it. If he had prevaricated about it, I'd never have forgiven him."

After this Adrian did not dare to confess. It was too bad. Here were both his uncle and Dora admiring Peter for his poems, and crediting Peter with candor and courage. He was to lose both fame and Dora! It was certainly too much. A sudden thought struck him. He went to town, called on Peter, and, as the police reports say, "made a communication" to him.

"It makes me look a scoundrel," objected Peter.

"Two hundred—at six months," suggested Adrian.

"And she is a nice girl—— No, I'm dashed——"

"A monkey at three!" cried Adrian.

"Done!" said Peter.

It was a sad tale of depravity on one side, and of self-sacrificing friendship on the other, that Mr. Pottles and Dora Chatterton listened to that evening.

"He had made," said Adrian sadly, "a deliberate attempt to rob me of my fame before, and he repeated it. And yet, uncle, an old friend—boyhood's companion—how could I betray him? It was weak, but I could not. I stood by, and let him deceive you."

"You're a noble fellow," said Mr. Pottles, in tones of emotion.

"Indeed, yes," said Dora, with an adoring glance.

"There, let us say no more about it," pursued Adrian magnanimously. "I have my reward," and he returned Dora's glance behind Mr. Pottles' broad back.

The next time he met Peter, he said, "I am really immensely indebted to you, old fellow. My uncle has come down handsome, and if the monkey now would be conv——"

"By Gad, yes!" said Peter. He took it in crisp notes, and carefully pocketed them.

"And is Miss Dora kind?" he asked.

"She's an angel."

"And you are generally prosperous?"

"Thanks to you, my dear old friend."

"Then," said Peter, producing a piece of paper from his pocket, "you might persuade your publishers to withdraw this beastly thing." It was a writ, and it claimed an injunction to restrain Peter from claiming the authorship of "To Lalage."

"Then you've been publicly claiming it?"

"I had to keep up the illusion, Adrian. Do me justice."

"But," said Adrian, "how, Peter—how does it happen that the writ is dated the day before we went to Clapham?"

He paused. Peter grinned uneasily. A light broke in on Adrian.

"Why," he exclaimed, "you're the villain who——"

"Exactly. Wonderfully provident of me, wasn't it? What, you're not going?"

"Never let me see your face again," said Adrian. "I have done with you."

He rushed out. Peter whistled gently, and said to himself, "Not a bad deal! He must stop the action, or the old man will twig."

Then he whistled again, and added, "Glad I got it in notes. He'd have stopped a check."

A third time he whistled, and chuckled and said, "Now, I wonder if old Adrian'll make five hundred and fifty out of it! Not a bad deal, Peter, my boy!"

MIDDLETON'S MODEL.

MIDDLETON was doing very well; everybody admitted that—some patronizingly, others enviously. And yet Middleton aimed high. He eschewed pot-boilers, and devoted himself to important subject pictures, often of an allegorical description. Nevertheless, his works sold, and that so well that Middleton thought himself justified in taking a wife. Here, again, good fortune attended him. Miss Angela Dove was fair to see, possessed of a nice little income, and, finally, a lady of taste, for she accepted Middleton's addresses. Decidedly a lucky fellow all round was Middleton. But, in spite of all his luck, his face was clouded with care as he sat in his studio one summer evening. Three months before he had been the recipient of a most flattering commission from that wealthy and esteemed connoisseur the Earl of Moneyton. The earl desired two panels for his hall. "I want," he wrote, "two full-length female figures—the one representing Heavenly Love, the other Earthly Love. Not a very new subject, you will say; but I have a fancy for it, and I can rely on your talent to impart freshness even to a well-worn theme."

Of course there was no difficulty about Heavenly Love. Angela filled the bill (the expression was Middleton's own) to a nicety. Her pretty golden hair, her sweet smile, her candid blue eyes, were exactly what was wanted. Middleton clapped on a pair of wings, and felt that he had done his duty. But when he came to Earthly Love the path was not so smooth. The earl demanded the acme of physical beauty, and that was rather hard to find. Middleton tried all the models in vain; he frequented the theaters and music-halls to no purpose; he tried to combine all the beauties of his acquaintance in one harmonious whole, but they did not make what tea-dealers call a "nice blend." Then he tried to evolve Earthly Love out of his own consciousness, but he could get nothing there but Angela again; and although he did violence to his feelings by giving her black hair and an evil cast in her eye, he knew that, even thus transformed, she would not satisfy the earl. Middleton was in despair; his reputation was at stake. The thought of Angela could not console him.

"I'd give my soul for a model!" cried he, flinging aside his pencil in despair.

At this moment he heard a knock at the door. He existed on the charwoman system, and after six o'clock in the evening had to open his own door. A lady stood outside, and a neat brougham was vanishing round the corner. Even in the darkness Middleton was struck by the grace and dignity of his visitor's figure.

"Mr. Middleton's, is it not?" she asked, in a very sweet voice.

Middleton bowed. It was late for a call, but if the lady ignored that fact, he could not remind her of it. Fortunately there was no chance of Angela coming at such an hour. He led the way to his studio.

"May I ask," he began, "to what I am indebted for this honor?"

"I see you like coming to business directly," she answered, her neatly gloved hands busy unpinning her veil. She seemed to find the task a little difficult.

"You see, it's rather late," said Middleton.

"Not at all. I am only just up. Well, then, to business. I hear you want a model for an Earthly Love."

"Exactly. May I ask if you———"

"If I am a model? Oh, now and then—not habitually."

"You know my requirements are somewhat hard to fulfill?"

"I can fulfill them," and she raised her veil. She certainly could. She realized his wildest dreams—the wildest dream of poets and painters since the world began. Middleton stood half-stupefied before her.

"Well, shall I do?" she asked, turning her smile on him.

Middleton felt as if it were a battery of guns, as he answered that he would be the happiest painter in the world if she would honor him.

"Head only, of course," she continued.

"Of course," said he hastily; "unless, that is, you will give me hands and arms too."

"I think not. My hands are not so good." And she glanced at her kid gauntlets with a smile.

"And—er—as to terms?" he stammered.

"Oh, the usual terms," she answered briskly.

Middleton hinted at pre-payment.

"I'm not allowed to take that," she said. "Come, I will ask for what I want when the time comes. You won't refuse me?"

"It's a little vague," he said, with an uneasy laugh.

"Oh, I can go away." And she turned toward the door.

"Whatever you like," he cried hastily.

"Ah, that's better. I shall not take anything of great value."

She gave him her hand. He ventured on a slight pressure. The lady did not seem to notice it, and her hand lay quite motionless in his.

"To-morrow, then?" he said.

"Yes. I won't trouble you to call a cab. I shall walk."

"Have you far to go?"

"Oh, some little way; but it's an easy road."

"Can't I escort you?"

"Not to-night. Some day, I hope"—and she stepped into the street and disappeared round the corner.

Punctually the next day she reappeared. Apart from her incomparable beauty —and every time she came, Middleton was more convinced that it was incomparable—she was a charming companion. She was very well read, and her knowledge of the world was wonderful.

"I wish it wasn't rude to ask your age!" he exclaimed one day.

"Ah, I am older than I look. My work keeps me young."

"Are you very busy, then?"

"I am always busy. But I don't grudge the time I give to you. No, don't thank me. I am to be paid, you know." And she laughed merrily. If there were a flaw in her, it was her laugh. Middleton thought it rather a cruel laugh.

"Do you know," he resumed, "you have never told me your name yet."

"I am here *incognita*."

"You will tell me some day?"

"Yes, you shall know some day."

"Before we part forever?"

"Perhaps we shall not part—forever."

Middleton said he hoped not; but what would Angela say?

"My name is not so pretty a one as your *fiancée's*," the lady continued.

"How do you know I am engaged?"

"I always know that sort of thing. It's so useful. Angela Dove, isn't it?"

"Yes; I hope you like it?"

"To be candid, not very much. It happens to have unpleasant associations."

It was fortunate that Angela was staying out of town. Middleton felt that the two ladies would not have got on well together; and—— He checked himself in shame; for his thought had been that not even for Angela could he send the stranger away. Middleton struggled against the treacherous passion that grew upon him; but he struggled in vain. He was guilty of postponing the finishing of his panel as long as he could. At last the lady grew impatient.

"I shall not come after to-day," she announced. "You can finish it to-day."

"Oh, hardly!" he protested.

"I'll stay late; but I can't come again."

Middleton worked hard, and by evening the panel was finished.

"A thousand thanks," he said. "And now you'll have something to eat, won't you?"

She agreed, and they sat down to a merry meal. The lady surpassed herself in brilliancy, and her mad gayety infected Middleton. Forgetful of his honor and allegiance, he leaned over to toast his guest, with a passionate gaze in his eyes. Insensibly the evening sped away; suddenly the clock struck twelve.

"I am going now," she said.

"Ah, you won't leave me!" cried Middleton.

"For the moment."

"But when shall I see you again?"

"As soon as you like, but not later than you must."

"You are charmingly mysterious. Tell me where you are going?"

"To my home."

"If you won't come to me, I shall come to you," he insisted.

"Yes, you will come to me," she answered, smiling.

"And we shall be together?"

"Yes."

"As long as ever I like?"

"Yes—longer."

"Impossible! Eternity would not be too long."

"*Nous verrons*," said she, with a laugh.

"At least you will write? You'll send me your picture?"

"I never write, and you have my picture."

"And another in my heart," he cried hotly.

"I have tried to put it there."

"But give me some token—anything—a ribbon—a glove—anything."

"Well, let it be a glove. As I go I will give you a glove."

She rose from her chair and rested her right hand on the table.

"Till we meet again!" she said.

"I am yours for ever!" he cried, seizing her hand.

"True! true!" she answered triumphantly. "You are mine forever!" and with a sudden movement she drew her arm away from him and left on the table—her glove, was it, or her hand? It seemed her very hand! and as Middleton looked up he had a vision of a blood-red claw shaken in his face, and devilish laughter rattled in his ears. The lady was gone, and Middleton fell full length on his studio floor.

Middleton is a very devoted husband to Angela Dove. When he is well and cheerful, he blames himself for having made love to a model, and laughs at himself for having been fool enough to fancy—well, all sorts of rubbish. But when he is out of sorts he does not like to be complimented on his figure of Earthly Love, and he gives a shudder if he happens to come across an article which lies hidden in his cupboard—a perfect model of the human hand covered with black kid; the model is hollow, and there is a curious black mark inside it.

And the earl? The earl was delighted with the panel.

"Was she a professional model?" he asked.

"She made it a matter of business with me," said Middleton uneasily. It was one of his bad days.

"I must know that girl," continued the earl, with a cunning look in his eye.

"I expect you will some day."

"What's her name?"

"I don't know. She didn't tell me."

"Didn't she sign anything when you paid her?"

"I haven't paid her yet."

"But you're going to?"

"I—I suppose so," answered Middleton.

"Well, you'll find out who she is then. And, I say, Middleton, just let me know."

"I will if I can—unless you've found it out before."

The earl took up his hat with a sigh.

"A glorious creature!" he said. "I hope I shall see her sometime."

"I think it's very likely, my lord," said Middleton.

"Have you any notion where she comes from?"

Middleton compromised. He said he understood that the lady was from Monte Carlo.

MY ASTRAL BODY.

THERE'S no doubt at all about it," said the rajah, relighting his cigar.

"It's perfectly easy, if you know how to do it. The skepticism of the West is nothing less than disgusting."

The rajah had come to Oxford to complete his education and endue himself with the culture of Europe; and he sat in my rooms, in a frock-coat of perfect cut (he always wore a frock-coat), smoking one of my weeds and drinking a whisky-and-soda. The rajah took to European culture with avidity, and I have very little doubt that he learned many new things with which it might or might not be expedient to acquaint his fellow-countrymen and subjects when he returned to India. But all the intellectual interests of Oxford were not strong enough to wean him from his love for the ancient lore of his own country, and he was always ready to expound the hidden wisdom of the East to any inquiring spirit. As soon as I found this out, I cultivated his acquaintance sedulously; for, in common with all intelligent men of the present day, I took a keen interest in that strange learning which seemed to give its possessors such extraordinary powers.

"Can you do it?" I asked.

"I should hope so," said the rajah contemptuously. "If I couldn't do that, I'd turn Mahommedan."

"I wish you'd teach me."

The rajah took in a deep puff of smoke. "You're sure you could manage it?" he asked.

"I beg your pardon?"

"Well, of course, like anything else, an astral body must be treated with tact, or it gets out of hand."

"Does it?"

"Why, yes; you must be firm and yet kind. Don't let it take liberties, or you don't know where it will land you. I rather doubt if I ought to show you."

I implored him to do so. I was young, rash, self-confident, and I thought I could manage an astral body as easily as I did the dean.

"Don't blame me if you find it too much for you, that's all," said the rajah. "And of course you must promise not to tell anyone."

"Oh, must I?"

"Yes, you must; because it's quite irregular in me to show you like this. You ought, by rights, you know, to go to Thibet for seven years."

"That would be rather a bore."

"Beastly," said the rajah; "but of course they insist on it, because they get the fees."

He swore me to secrecy by all manner of oaths, and lastly on my word as a gentleman; and then he showed me. I practiced all that evening, and was tolerably proficient by the time the rajah knocked out his last pipe and went off to bed. I must not tell how it is done, as I promised not to; besides, if anyone reads this narrative through, he will never want to know.

At first it was very convenient. I always used to project it to chapel instead of going myself. It did capitally there, because it had only to behave itself and hold its tongue. At lectures it was a failure; it was such an inattentive beggar that its notes were worth nothing. And it was no sort of use in the Torpid; I was told that I should be turned out if I went on "sugaring" like that—there's no pluck or endurance in these Orientals. On the whole, however, I was very well satisfied with it, and came to rely upon it more and more for all the unpleasant duties of life.

"Well, how do you like it?" asked the rajah one day in Quad.

"My dear fellow, it's splendid," I answered. "It's up in town, being measured for trousers, now. You can't think how much trouble it saves."

The rajah smiled and shook his head.

"Be moderate," he said. "You mustn't use it too much, or it'll presume on it."

"Will it? What will it do?"

"Why, if it's always being projected, it's as likely as not it'll learn the trick of it, and take to projecting itself. Then you'll be left in the lurch."

"What shall I do then?"

"I don't see what you can do," said the rajah, scratching his head. "Of course, I should merely report it at headquarters; but you can't, because you've no business with it at all."

"Well, I shan't grudge it a holiday now and then," I said magnanimously.

The rajah was right. It did begin to take French leave. Several times when I wanted it I found it had, without a word of apology, projected itself off to Iffley or somewhere, and was not available. I spoke very severely to it. It said nothing, but listened with an unpleasant sort of smile. "We all have our duties," I remarked, "and yours is to be here"—and I pointed to my chest —"when you are wanted. You're as bad as a scout."

"I ought to have a little relaxation," it answered sulkily.

"I never heard of such a thing in connection with you. Isn't it enough for you to meditate in four dimensions when you're not at work? That would satisfy most people."

"It's all very well in Thibet," it grumbled; "but a fellow doesn't come to Oxford to do that."

"One would think you had nothing to do with me. You seem to forget that you are simply a projection of mine."

We had some high words and parted—I mean, united—in very bad temper with one another. It was in the middle of a most impertinent and positively threatening speech, when I terminated the interview by resuming it. It was very unreasonable and irritating, and I made up my mind to ask the rajah to speak to it the next morning. I had an engagement that evening, or I would have done it then. How I wish I had!

At half-past nine I went to an "At Home" at Professor Drayton's. As a rule, "At Homes" are dull; but I had a reason for going to this one. The professor had a very pretty daughter, and I was vain enough to think that my presence was welcome to her. In fact, we were great friends, and I had not been at the house a quarter of an hour before I had forgotten all my worries with my unruly Astral Body, and was sitting by Bessie in the small drawing room, enjoying myself immensely. Suddenly—mysteriously—I felt something like a violent push. Bessie vanished; the drawing room vanished; and I found myself in the High, standing in dripping rain, without a hat or coat. I stood still in bewilderment. What had happened? A moment later the proctor was upon me. I gave my name and college in a mechanical way, and he passed on, leaving me still standing in the rain. What had happened? Then it flashed across my mind. I understood its threats. It had projected me!

I woke up next morning, determined to have it out with it. I found, as I expected, that it had waited till I was asleep; then it slunk in and united without my knowing it. I went and paid my fine, and then, not waiting to breakfast, I proceeded to project it. It wouldn't move! I tried again and again. I had no more power over it than a child. I knew it was there; but I could not move it an inch. In wrath, I jumped up, seized my cap, and started for the rajah's rooms. The rogue saw what I was up to. I give you my word, I had not reached the door when it projected me most viciously, and I landed down in the Parks.

I was not to be beaten. I came back to college at a run, and made straight for the rajah's rooms. It was on the lookout for me. As I ran by my oak, which I had to pass, it rushed out on me, united, and projected me back again to Magdalen Bridge. This happened three times. Then I sat down in the Parks, just where I dropped, and acknowledged to myself that I was in a pretty fix.

I had a fearful week of it. Of course, wherever I was, it could unite at once by just thinking of me; and, directly it had united, it used, I believe out of pure malice, to project me somewhere where I did not want to go. It was lucky for me that it was new to the business; its powers were as yet very undeveloped, and, consequently, it did not carry very far. If it could, I am sure it would have sent me to the Antipodes; but as it was, I never went further than the University boat-house—a pretty tidy step on a bad morning. Still, it was improving; and I felt that I must act at once if I did not want to be a permanent wanderer on the face of the earth.

My only chance was to engross its attention in some way, so that it would forget me for a little while, and leave me free to speak to the rajah. I pinned all my hopes on the rajah. Well, one morning, about a week after it first projected me, I went for a walk in Christchurch Meadow. We were united, and it had actually left me in peace ever since breakfast. I hoped its better feelings were beginning to get the mastery of it, and, in order to see, I tried to project it. No, it wouldn't move! The creature was still recalcitrant.

Suddenly I saw Bessie Drayton just in front of me. In delight at seeing her, I forgot about it, and, quickening my pace, overtook her, and lifted my hat. She smiled divinely, saying, "Why, Mr. Nares, I just going to write——" At that moment, when I was listening to her sweet voice, it projected me! Could ill-nature go further? But, luckily, its mind was not really concentrated on what it was doing. I believe it was thinking of Bessie, and consequently it only carried about a hundred yards. I landed behind one of the big elms, where I lay *perdu* till it had gone by. It and Bessie passed me together, and it was grinning from ear to ear, and looked as pleased as Punch. And poor Bessie, who thought she was talking to me, was being most charming to it.

I did not waste time in swearing. I ran like the wind back to college, hoping that Bessie's society would prevent it coming after me till I had spoken to the rajah. I still retained one pull over it. In order to unite, it had to come where I was; it could not resume me from a distance, as I used to resume it; so if it united now it would have to leave Bessie.

By a blessed chance, the rajah was at home, and in trembling haste I poured my story into his ear. He burst out laughing.

"I was afraid of it!" he gasped, holding his sides. "How splendid!"

I restrained my annoyance, and after a time he became a little more grave.

"Do help me!" I urged. "It may unite at any moment, and project me the deuce knows where."

"Oh, it'll be all right with the young lady."

"Not for long. She's very particular, and won't let it walk far with her."

"Oh, then we must act. You don't feel it yet?"

"No; but do be quick!"

The rajah sported his oak, took off his coat, lay down on the floor, and went into strong convulsions.

I regretted putting him to so much trouble, but my need was urgent, and I knew that he was a good-natured man. Presently he cried (and I was just getting alarmed about him):

"Are you there, Nani-Tal?"

"Certainly," said an old white-haired gentleman, dressed in a sheet, who sat in the rajah's armchair.

"That's all right," said the rajah, getting up and putting on his coat. "You were very difficult."

"We're so busy just now," said Nani-Tal apologetically. "I'm demonstrating three nights a week, and the preparations take all my time."

"Well, you can't have a boom for nothing," said the rajah, smiling.

"I don't complain," said Nani-Tal; "I only mentioned it to excuse myself for keeping you waiting. I was in New York when you began materializing. It's a lively city."

"You must tell him all about it," said the rajah to me; "he won't be very hard on us."

Nani-Tal was, however, rather severe. He said it was too bad of the rajah. How were they to live, if that sort of thing went on? Then he turned to me, and added, "Of course you couldn't manage it. If you'd gone through the course, you would have been all right. But there, it's everything for nothing nowadays!"

"My friend couldn't go to Thibet."

"He might have paid the fees anyhow," grumbled Nani-Tal, "and taken correspondence lessons."

We smoothed him down with the promise of a handsome donation, and at last he consented to help us. It was only just in time, for at that very moment I felt my Astral Body uniting. A second later it made a violent effort to project me; of course, it saw Nani-Tal, and knew it was in for it. The old gentleman was too quick for it.

"Come out of that!" he cried imperiously, and the wretch stood in the middle of the room.

It did my heart good to hear Nani-Tal fall on the creature. After giving it no end of a lecture, he concluded, "And now, young man, you'll just go back to your jackal for a thousand years, and learn better manners."

The wretch protested; it asked for an elephant or even a tiger. Nani-Tal was obdurate.

"A jackal will just suit you," he said. "Be off!" The creature vanished. Simultaneously Nani-Tal began to disintegrate.

"Wait a bit!" cried the rajah.

"I can't. I'm summoned to St. James' Hall. There's a large audience, and the professor has been in convulsions seven minutes."

I tried to grasp his hand in thanks. "If you want another," he said, "you must go through the course—the full course. There's no other way. Let this be a lesson to you." And with this parting remark he disintegrated.

The rajah lit a cigar, and I, lighter at heart than I had been for many days, followed his example.

"It was wrong of me," said the rajah; "I won't do it again."

"It's a pity it turned out so badly," I remarked; "it was quite a comfort at first."

"They're all like that, unless you keep a tight hand on them. Shall you take the course?"

"Not I. I've had enough of it."

"Perhaps you're right. Excuse me; I have to go to the Deccan on business."

He fell back on the sofa, apparently in a trance, and I went off to the dean's lecture. It makes all the difference whether you know how to do a thing or not.

THE NEBRASKA LOADSTONE.

IF there was one man in college whom the rajah thoroughly and heartily detested, it was the captain of the boat club. He had many faults; he was very tall and powerful, and delighted in contrasting the English physique with that of inferior races; by which he meant, among others, the rajah's race. His manner was abrupt and overbearing, his laugh loud and unmusical. In fact, he grated horribly on the rajah; and it was merely the final straw when, in the exhilaration of a bump supper,—full, as the rajah remarked in disgust, of cow and strong drink,—he called that prince, in playful chaff, a "nigger." The rajah swore melodiously in Hindustani, and I saw that he meant to be revenged.

In those days the entertainment of the Nebraska Loadstone created a *furore*. Everybody went to see her, and everybody came away convinced that she possessed marvelous powers. Her peculiar gift—but everybody remembers the details of the performance, and how the tricks were finally, one by one, exposed, so that her adherents and believers were driven from one position to another, until at last they had to fall back on one single performance out of all those that the Loadstone gave, and maintain that on that occasion at least something unexplained and inexplicable did really happen. It is with the events of that particular evening that I am concerned. I think I can throw some light on them.

At first, however, there were many believers and few skeptics. The dean carefully pointed out that Plato nowhere denied the existence of odic force; and the bursar, who was generally supposed to be little better than an atheist, declared that Spencer in one passage impliedly asserted it; even the warden, in his sermon, told us that it was better, according to Bacon, to believe two errors than refuse one truth—which was, to say the least of it, sitting on the fence. But none of these authorities shook the robust skepticism of the captain of the boat club. He knew a conjurer, and the conjurer had told him how it was done, and he was going to expose the Loadstone.

"But why haven't you?" I urged. "She's been here a week."

"He will not be too hard on her at first," said the rajah, with a little sneer.

"I'll bust her up this very night," said Waterer. "I would have done it before, only I was gated."

The excuse was good, and Waterer departed, full of boastings and self-confidence, to gather together a large number of the noisy men, and make a pleasant party to "guy" the unhappy Loadstone. I stayed to smoke a pipe with the rajah.

"Of course she's a fraud," said he; "and I believe that animal really has got hold of the right explanation."

"I shall go and see it," I announced.

After a moment's silent smoking, the rajah looked up with a twinkle in his eye. "So shall I—if niggers are admitted."

After hall, he and I set out together for the town hall. We found the first two rows of stalls occupied by Waterer and his friends. They were all in evening dress, and had obviously dined—not in hall. The rajah and I seated ourselves just behind them. The room was full, and the feats were being most successful; each was followed by general applause, broken only by some gibes from our friends in front. These latter grew so pronounced that the Loadstone's manager at last came forward and pointedly invited one of the scoffers to submit himself to experiment.

Now was Waterer's chance. He rose in the majesty of his bulk, walked on to the platform, and said in a loud voice, as he settled himself on a chair, "If the lady can move me one foot from this chair, I'll give her a pony!"

The Loadstone advanced and began to paw him about in her usual fashion. Waterer, who was sober enough to have lost nothing but his shyness, was apparently too many for her. He was immovable; and cries of, "Now then! when are you going to begin?" and so on, became audible. Two or three minutes passed, and the Loadstone turned with a gesture of despair toward her manager.

"I can't——" she began.

I jumped to my feet, crying, "Wait a minute! Look!"

For even as she spoke, there was what is scientifically called a solution of continuity between Waterer and his chair. Still in a sitting posture, but sitting on nothing, he was at least two inches from the wicker-work of the chair. I glanced from him to the rajah. That extraordinary man was in deep, placid, profound slumber. I jogged his elbow and pinched his arm; he showed no consciousness whatever. I looked at the Loadstone. She was standing motionless on the stage about a yard from Waterer, with one hand outstretched toward him, and her eyes fixed on his ascending figure; for Waterer was gradually, slowly, steadily mounting in his strange journey. He was now a foot from his chair, still in a sitting position—and up, up, up he was going. The wretch was white as a sheet, and gasping with fright and bewilderment. Thunders of applause burst from the audience. It was again and again renewed; but the Loadstone did not, as her custom was, bow and smile in response. She still stood motionless, and Waterer still ascended.

At last, at a height of fully twenty feet from the stage, he stopped. Simultaneously the Loadstone gave a loud shriek as she fell back into the arms of the manager—and the rajah awoke.

"I beg your pardon," he said politely; "I was drowsy. Anything going on?"

"No; he's stopped now," I answered, my eyes eagerly fixed on Waterer.

The rajah rose from his seat with a yawn. "There'll be nothing more to-night," he said. "Let's go home."

"Go home, man!—with that before our eyes!"

The rajah shrugged his shoulders.

"She won't do anything more," he repeated. "Look at her; she's quite done up."

And, indeed, the Loadstone looked half dead as she gazed fearfully up at Waterer. Her demeanor was not that of a triumphant performer.

"Do sit down," I urged; "we must see the end of it."

With a weary sigh, the rajah sat down, saying, "I'm not sure you will, you know."

While we talked, the audience grew impatient. However wonderful a feat may be, the public likes to have things kept moving. They thought Waterer had been in the air long enough, and there were cries of "That'll do! Let him down!" "Give us another."

The manager held a hasty conference with the Loadstone: he seemed to urge her; but she shook her head again and again, and would do nothing but lie back in a chair, and pass her hand to and fro over her head. The rajah looked at her with a slight smile. The clamor increased. I think a sort of panic—an angry panic—seized the audience.

"Bring him down! Bring him down!" they cried, pointing to the pallid Waterer, who sat as rigid as a trussed fowl.

After another despairing appeal to the Loadstone, the manager came forward and made a lame speech. The Loadstone was exhausted with her unparalleled exertions. She must rest; presently she would bring him down. Then Waterer's friends arose and ascended the platform. They walked about, they stood on one another's shoulders; they made it clear that no cords held Waterer. A pair of steps was called for and brought. Placed on a sturdy table, they just enabled a man to reach Waterer's feet. One mounted amidst intense excitement. Turning to the rajah, I exclaimed, "Look!"

He was asleep again; and the Loadstone stood stiffly upright, beckoning toward Waterer. Slowly and gradually he descended, leaving the man on the ladder grasping at empty air, till he sat again on his seat. The applause burst out, and the Loadstone sank back in a faint on the floor. The rajah awoke, and the manager dropped the curtain, hiding the Loadstone, Waterer, and his friends from our view.

"Give me your arm," said the rajah; "I am tired." I escorted him to a cab, and we drove home.

The Loadstone gave no performance the next evening: she was too fatigued; and Waterer was absent from the boat and from the sight of men two days. When he reappeared he made no reference to his friend the conjurer. He slunk about the Quad, looking very pale and upset. I met him once, when I was with the rajah, on our way to lecture. The rajah smiled urbanely at Waterer, and said to me, when he had passed:

"It's such a rude thing to call a gentleman a nigger, isn't it?"

Waterer has not done it again. And the Loadstone never did that trick again. She took the pony, though. The manager called on Waterer, and asked for a check. I think that incident pleased the rajah most of all.

"It is a ready utilization of the unexpected," he remarked, "which does our friend much credit."

A SUCCESSFUL REHEARSAL.

MR. ALOYSIUS TAPPENHAM, of Stamford Road, was a dealer in frauds. It must not be understood from this statement that he was either a company-promoter or the manager of a philanthropic undertaking. On the contrary, he was as honest a man of business as you would find in London, and he earned his living by discovering and introducing new attractions in the shape of "Wonders," "Phenomenons," and so forth. The music-halls were Mr. Tappenham's best customers, and when he successfully launched a new impostor, he reaped a handsome return in the way of commissions on the salary of the impostor and the profits of the *entrepreneur*. All his *protégés* were a success—a fact chiefly to be attributed to his unvarying habit of insisting that he himself should be shown "how it was done." He promised and observed absolute secrecy; but, as he always said, he could not properly judge of the merit of any particular fraud, unless he were allowed a private view of the machinery by which it was worked. Some few years ago, in the very prime of life and the full tide of a profitable trade, Mr. Tappenham suddenly retired from business. This was the reason:

One day Mr. Tappenham discovered a treasure in the shape of a very attractive young lady whose name was Hopkins, but who proposed to call herself Mlle. Claire.Claire was hardly suitable to the music-halls; Mr. Tappenham thought that she was above that, and proposed to "run" her himself in Bond Street, on half-profit terms. Her specialty was the production of any spirit you liked to order. She received in a dimly lighted room; you told her who you were, and whose spirit you wished to interview, and forthwith, without any nonsense of hand-holding or table-turning, she caused to appear a shadowy yet clearly perceptible figure which was exactly like the person you named, spoke with that person's voice, and exhibited full—or reasonably full—knowledge of everything which that person, and that person only, might be expected to know.

Mr. Tappenham was much struck with the dexterity of this performance. Of course, when explained, it resolved itself into some clever optical illusion, a little ventriloquism, and a good deal of tact in returning to the inquirer in another form information pumped out of him beforehand. The materials were simple, the result was highly artistic; and Mr. Tappenham determined to furnish the only thing needful to set London aflame with the new marvel—namely, capital. However, before taking the last irreparable step, he decided on a final trial. He prepared the *mise-en-scène* with due completeness, and invited Mlle. Claire to experiment on himself.

"Consider me as one of the public," he said, "and give me a hair-raiser."

Mlle. Claire protested that he was too much behind the scenes; but, on being pressed, she consented to try, and asked Mr. Tappenham to name his spirit.

He thought for a moment, and then said, "When I was a young man, I knew a girl called Nellie Davies—a pretty girl, my dear. I dare say I didn't treat her over well; but that's neither here nor there. Let's have her."

Clever little Mlle. Claire asked a question or two—and Mr. Tappenham admired the neat and apparently undesigned nature of her questions—and then set to work, after drawing the curtains a shade closer, and turning the light a trifle lower.

Mr. Tappenham sat comfortably in an armchair, his hands crossed over his white waistcoat, and a smile of satisfaction on his face. Presently the shadowy shape began to form itself a yard or two from Mr. Tappenham.

"Capital, capital!" he chuckled. "That'll fetch 'em." The shape grew more definite.

"Will that do?" asked Mlle. Claire triumphantly. "Is it like?"

"Now, by Jove, it is rather! Make it speak."

Mlle. Claire laughed, and, projecting her voice to the shape, began in low, sweet, sad tones. "You summoned me. What do you desire of your dead friend?"

She stopped, laughing again, and said, "It's no use, when you're up to it beforehand."

Mr. Tappenham did not answer her. He sat looking at the shape, and seemed to be listening intently.

"Shall I go on?" she inquired.

Mr. Tappenham took no notice.

"What's the matter with him?" thought Mlle. Claire. "I shan't go on if he's not listening."

Assuming her pretended voice again, she said, "I will try to forgive. Farewell, farewell!" and, with a merry, boisterous laugh, she displaced the arrangement which produced the illusion, and said to Mr. Tappenham:

"Now are you satisfied?" Then she added, in a tone of surprise, "Whatever is the matter?" For, as she looked, the expression of his face changed from attention to surprise, from surprise to uneasiness. He turned to her and said, with a forced smile, "It's too clever—a sight too clever. That'll do; stop it, please."

"Stop it?"

"Yes. I've had enough. It's—it's damned absurd, but it's getting on my nerves. Stop it, I say—stop it!" His voice rose at the end almost into a cry.

"Why, I have stopped it this three minutes!" she answered in surprise.

His eyes had wandered from her to where the shape had been; but at her last words he turned to her again with a start. "What? No, no! No nonsense! Come, now, be a good girl and stop it. I've had enough."

"Are you drunk?" asked Mlle. Claire impatiently. "It's all over."

"I won't be made a fool of," said he angrily. "Stop it, or not a farthing do you get from me."

"Heaven bless the man, he's mad!" exclaimed the lady, who began to be a little uncomfortable herself. It is an eerie thing to see a man looking hard at— nothing, and listening intently to—nothing.

Suddenly he jumped up and ran toward Mlle. Claire. He seized her by the arm, and cried, "Stop, you little devil, stop! Do you want to madden me? I never did it, I never did. At least, I never meant it—so help me, God, I never meant it."

"Mr. Tappenham, you're dreaming. There's nothing there. I'm saying nothing."

"She's coming! she's coming!" he cried. "Take her away! take her away!"

Mlle. Claire looked at his face. Then she too gave a shriek of fright, and, hiding her face in her hands, sank on the floor, sobbing. She saw nothing. But what was that face looking at?

As for Mr. Tappenham, he fled into the corner of the room. And when Mlle. Claire recovered herself enough to draw back the curtains, and let in the blessed sun, he lay on the floor like a man dead.

Mlle. Claire was a good girl. She had a mother and two little brothers to keep: so she stuck to the business; but she never liked it very much after that day. Mr. Tappenham could afford to retire, and he did retire. He lives very quietly, and gives large sums in charity. Mlle. Claire knows all the tricks that ever were invented; she is a thorough-going little skeptic, and believes in nothing that she does not see, and in very little of what she does. Therefore she merely exemplifies feminine illogicality when she thinks to herself, as she cannot help thinking now and then:

"I wonder what he did to Nellie Davies!"

She told me about it, and I believed her when she said that she was not playing a trick on Mr. Tappenham. But perhaps she was deceiving me also; if so, that is an explanation.

I repeated the story to a scientific man. He said that it furnished an interesting instance of the permanence of an optical impression after the removal of the external excitant. That is another explanation.

Or it may have been the working of conscience: that is an explanation in a way, though an improbable one, because, in spite of many opportunities, Mr. Tappenham's conscience had never given him any inconvenience before. It has since.

THE END.

Printed in Poland
by Amazon Fulfillment
Poland Sp. z o.o., Wrocław